Putting the War to Rest

Do you find that dieting is a struggle? Have you started diets with great hope only to find yourself giving up due to temptation? Do you feel deprived, frustrated, and hopeless in your failed attempts to reach your ideal image? Do you feel you lack control and will-power? You're not alone. Even successful dieters complain of an underlying struggle to hold onto their achievement. As a counselor and health educator who has worked with eating disorders and overweight since 1982, Dr. Constance Kirk has felt some of the same frustration and hopelessness you have. Why? The dismally low success rate of only 5 per cent for losing weight and maintaining ideal weight is not because the traditional approaches of diet and exercise do not work. It is because the person fails to *act* in consistently positive ways.

This book is an extension of a workbook used with clients for weight and body composition problems, conerns, and/or goals. It is a compilation of cognitive strategies involving imagery and language which serves to lead the reader in understanding, carrying out, and intepreting each strategy. Instead of being "counselor dependent," it stands on its own. It is written in an easily understandable, conversational style, as though Dr. Kirk were personally speaking to you.

It is not at all surprising that when you suffer from feelings of deprivation and frustration that you are strongly motivated to end that pain. As long as you experience healthy eating and exercise as punishing, you are set up for failure. The purpose of this book is to guide you in ending the struggle, the pain. It "tames the diet dragon," paving the way for you to succeed with greater joy and ease.

About the Author

Dr. Kirk is an Assistant Professor at the University of Wisconsin, Whitewater. She earned her doctorate in health education at the University of Northern Colorado. A health educator for 15 years, she has designed and facilitated seminars in Weight Dynamics, imagery for weight control and imagery for healing.

To Write to the Author

We cannot guarantee that every letter written to the author can be answered, but all will be forwarded. Both the author and the publisher appreciate hearing from readers, learning of your enjoyment and benefit from this book. Llewellyn also publishes a bimonthly news magazine with news and reviews of practical esoteric studies and articles helpful to the student, and some readers' questions and comments to the author may be answered through this magazine's columns if permission to do so is included in the original letter. The author sometimes participates in seminars and workshops, and dates and places are announced in The Llewellyn New Times. To write to the author, or to ask a question, write to:

Constance C. Kirk
c/o The Llewellyn New Times
P.O. Box 64383-372, St. Paul, MN 55164-0383
Please enclose a self-addressed, stamped envelope
for reply, or $1.00 to cover costs.

Llewellyn's Self-Empowerment Series

TAMING
THE DIET
DRAGON

Using Language & Imagery for Weight Control and Body Transformation

Dr. Constance C. Kirk

1992
Llewellyn Publications
St. Paul, Minnesota 55164-0383, U.S.A.

FIRST EDITION

Cover painting by Randy Asplund-Faith
Illustration of pituitary gland by Andrew Gillham

Library of Congress Cataloging in Publication Data
Kirk, Constance C. (Constance Carroll), 1945-
    Taming the diet dragon : Using language and imagery
 for weight control and body transformation /
    Constance C. Kirk.
       p. cm. — (Llewellyn's self-empowerment series)
    Includes bibliographical references.
    ISBN 0-87542-372-8 (pbk.) : $9.95
    1. Reducing—Psychological aspects   2. Imagery
(Psychology)   3. Body image.   I. Title.   II. Series.
RM222.2.K545   1992
613.2'5—dc20   92 727
                                                          CIP

Llewellyn Publications
A Division of Llewellyn Worldwide, Ltd.
P.O. Box 64383, St. Paul, MN 55164 0383

About Llewellyn's Self-Empowerment Series

We all desire to live a "full life," one that we can look back on with no regrets. Yet many of us live from day to day feeling that "something" in our life is missing, or that we have become a victim of circumstances which make happiness impossible.

Ironically, even when we desire to make a positive change in our life, we often stick with situations or behaviors that are unhealthy for us, be they bad relationships, unfulfilling work, or addictions to food, money, sex, or drugs.

The greatest barrier to human growth is the illusion of helplessness and powerlessness. It is the illusion that we have no choices in life.

Nothing could be further from the truth. Everyone has inherent resources to succeed if he or she learns to tap into them. And that's where self-empowerment comes in.

To empower yourself means to make choices to improve your life with commitment, style and joyfulness. It is reclaiming your own creative power to change, to love and nurture yourself, and to persevere in obtaining your goals. It is ultimately about creating your own reality.

Llewellyn's Self-Empowerment Series gives you a direct opportunity to improve yourself and your life through practical, step-by-step guidance from people who have mastered the techniques they share. It challenges you to be the best you can be, to *experience change,* not just read about it. It challenges you to surrender old assumptions and self-deceit in favor of growth and honesty. It challenges you to affect deep and powerful changes in your life.

Congratulations. You have already taken the first, most important step toward reclaiming your own amazing power. You have chosen to read this book. A full and rewarding life is yours for the living.

Permissions

Acknowledgements

I thank all my teachers, many of whom turned up in the most unlikely places. Students, clients, and research "subjects" provided much of the material for this work. It would have been impossible without them. Combined, they helped bring fragmented bits and pieces of information into an integrated whole. It is my hope that their trust, faith, and courage will inspire the same attributes in others.

A very special thanks:

To my Dad, Leland Kirk, who valued and nurtured my imagination.

To Paula Hayford, Edee Wright, and Carol Bedwell for their continued support and love.

To Colin Rose who helped transform subconscious doubt into conscious positive expectation, a special gift;

To Judy Fulop, Nicholas Brink, and Gary Anderson for their feedback and suggestions concerning the original manuscript.

To the "original" volunteers who participated in the first pilot study on imagery and metabolism as well as to all the other people who assisted in other phases of the research, Linda Schuettpelz, Chris Charlier, and Jan Wade. Mercy Medical Center (Oshkosh) provided equipment and space. A University of Wisconsin-Oshkosh Faculty Development grant funded the research.

Dedication

I wish to dedicate this book to
those people whose spark of hope
in the midst of pain and despair
serve as models of courage
for us all.

Table of Contents

Introduction   xiii

Part One: Languaging   1

  Chapter 1: Languaging:
    The Key to Unlocking Limitless Possibilities   3

  Chapter 2: Designer Affirmations:
    Creating Your Own Growth Language   17

  Chapter 3: Goal Setting   47

  Chapter 4: The Working Ideal:
    Building Motivational Muscle   65

Part Two: Imagery   79

  Chapter 5: Imagery: The Power Source   81

  Chapter 6: Levels of Imagery   89

  Chapter 7: Assets and Liabilities:
    Enhancing the Power of Imagery   125

  Chapter 8: The Personal Power Pack:
    Using Language and Imagery Together   137

Part Three: Experience   161

  Chapter 9: Savoring   163

  Chapter 10: Listening to the Body   181

  Chapter 11: Conclusion   201

Appendix A: Interpreting and Transforming
  Negative Language   207
Appendix B: Experience with Imagery   217
References   227

INTRODUCTION

The dragon is an age-old symbol of the highest
spiritual essence, embodying wisdom, strength,
and the divine power of transformation.
—Peter Matthiessen

The highest love a person can have for you is to wish
for you to evolve into the best person you can be.
—David Viscott

Even if you're on the right track you'll get run
over if you just sit there.
—Will Rogers

. . . as the person seeks a quick fix, he also circum-
vents his own growth.
—Marsha Sinetar

Introduction

I went on a diet for two weeks and you know what I lost? Fourteen days.

—*Totie Fields*

The late comedian, Totie Fields, expressed the frustration of the thousands of dieters who fail in their attempts to lose weight and keep it off. Ninety-five per cent fail. Ninety per cent of all females and 50 per cent of all males over 30 have been on at least one reduction diet, and yet 40 per cent of the United States population is overweight. Obesity has become one of most serious nutritional/health problems of our time.

Why are we such dismal failures when the solution is so obviously simple—diet and exercise? It is not from lack of trying. Diet books and cookbooks outsell all other categories. We spend millions of dollars on weight control programs, diet aids, diet pills, diet foods and drinks, jaw wiring, intestinal bypasses, stomach stapling, and liposuction. Not only does obesity threaten physical health, but also the concern over fat and food has become an obsession which consumes the vital life energy of thousands of people. Psychic energy is depleted to the point where there is little left for other pursuits, a tragic waste of human resources. Life was meant for more important things.

As a health educator who has counselled hundreds of people, I believe that most of the 95 per cent who fail are simply looking in the wrong places for answers. It seems overwhelmingly evident that, if one diet fails, and then the next, and the next, ad infinitum, that the answer does not lie in the diet. As long as one stays on a diet and exercises, one loses or maintains weight—well, at least most of the time. And if you are one of those who cannot lose, the problem will be addressed later . . . with solutions.

We need to figure out how to keep doing what we need to be doing. We need to start looking at positive behavioral change as gifts to ourselves rather than an endless succession of personal sacrifices and deprivation. We need to enjoy the process of affirming and nurturing ourselves. And we need to make the process a natural one. In short, we need to redirect the energy squandered on internal conflict. We tame the diet dragon; we do not kill it.

The puritanical work ethnic we have inherited seduces us into believing that to be successful all we have to do is work harder. The problem lies in the fact that we work harder doing the same thing when we need to learn to do something different.

Bandler and Grinder (1979), in the book *Frogs into Princes*, observed the differences in behavior between rats and human beings from their maze running experiments. When the experimenters removed the rewards for running (cheese for rats and five-dollar bills for humans), they found that, after a few runs, the rats stopped running. "However, the humans never stopped . . . They are still there . . . They break into the labs at night" (p. 13). "*If they* [human beings] *find something they can do that doesn't work, they do it again . . . If what you do doesn't work, do something else*" (pp. 12-13). Instead of dieting, do something different. The answer lies within, not without.

This book is about doing something different. It is about changing the way you think, which in turn changes the way you behave. Further, it changes your physiology. It is about removing obstacles and barriers. It is about learning to nurture and love yourself. It ultimately is about creating your own reality and fulfilling your best potential.

You see, the answers to the perplexities of overweight are not in a special diet but in you. Obesity, overfat, and eating disorders are signs and symptoms of other underlying and perhaps more serious problems which are concerns both for the individual and our society. The root of the problem is within you, but the good news is that the root of the solution is within you too. I am absolutely convinced that everyone, without exception, has the inherent resources to succeed if one but learns to tap into those resources. My objective is to guide you in the discovery of these resources.

This book is about reclaiming the power of choice which is your inherent right and privilege. It is about making the choices you truly desire to make effortlessly. It is about enacting positive, self-nurturing choice as a naturally occurring process rather than struggling. The never-ending battle can cease. We will, in partnership, TAME THE DIET DRAGON.

The essence of this work is tapping into and making available your resources through discovery, experience, and application. The process is fun, but it involves an investment of time and energy. It may also be frightening and uncomfortable at times because it involves surrendering old assumptions and self-deceit in favor of growth and honesty. However, the skills and information you learn can change your life in all its dimensions. Ideal weight is a by-product which naturally comes about through making choices to improve the quality of your life with a sense of commitment, style, and joyfulness. Not many people think of losing weight as a joyful process! The payoff is worth the price 100-fold.

When I was six years old, I had a friend, Earl, who was four. One afternoon Earl was sitting in the backyard digging a hole in the dirt with a spoon. Satisfied that the hole was deep enough, he proceeded to drop a seed in the hole, cover it with dirt, and place a large brick on top of it. My father, having observed Earl's handiwork, exclaimed, "Earl, that will never grow!" Earl looked up at my father from the dust and stated emphatically, "Yes it will. It will grow up to be real strong!"

In the years that I have been working with weight control, I have been struck with the similarities between Earl's practices in horticulture and human behavior. All the potentialities of Earl's plant were housed in a tiny seed. Everything that the plant could be was contained within the genetic code of the DNA. Whether or not those potentialities were expressed depended upon whether the soil and climatic conditions were favorable for that particular kind of plant. In the case of the seed, luck played its part. Unfortunately for that particular seed , it had the bad luck to fall into Earl's hands. Earl's sense of logic was unfavorable for nurturing growth.

Like the plant, the expression of human potential is dependent upon one's genetic composition and a myriad of environmental variables. However, people possess the power of will and choice with which to nurture or destroy themselves. Although there are many factors which we are virtually powerless to affect, many other factors influencing our individual growth are within our power to alter to a significant degree. One of the most effective ways to learn how to nurture ourselves is to observe and learn from people who are successful. One must ask the right questions. We are going to focus on and learn from the successful 5 per cent. And we will do it in a different way than one might expect.

Usually, when one meets someone who was successful with weight loss, the first question asked of the person is, "How did you do it?" One is asking for "the diet," or for the specifics of action. Seldom is the question, "What qualities do you have that allowed you to be successful?" Or, "How did you develop those qualities? How can I develop those or similar qualities?" Fortunately, there are some researchers who are asking the right questions and we will learn from them.

The most powerful insight leading to positive lifestyle change is the awareness that you have a choice. The greatest barrier to human growth is the illusion of helplessness and powerlessness. Putting on the mask of martyr and victim is not only a heavy burden, it is one of the most dangerous mental frameworks one can assume. Each time you play victim you literally give your power away. People even give their power away to inanimate objects, such as food. Food is nothing more than a mass of protoplasm on a plate, and yet people personify food to the point where one would believe the food jumped off the plate, forced its way into the mouth, and stormed into the stomach and fat cells. What is one to do? "I just smell food and gain weight."

Abdicating power is a supreme act of self-betrayal. Each time you relinquish taking responsibility for yourself, you lose an opportunity for self-nurturance and personal growth. The successful 5 per cent do not fall into these mental traps. They choose an attitude of faith rather than hopelessness, joy over sadness, victory over defeat.

All of these choices are manifestations of thought processes. A poignant example of life-affirming choice is illustrated in Victor Frankl's book, *Man's Search for Meaning*.

Victor Frankl was a psychiatrist who survived the hor-
rors of the Nazi concentration camps during World War II.
He observed that, when an inmate gave up, he would die
soon thereafter. He questioned why some gave up while
others did not. Despite the despicable and most degrading
of all circumstances for humans to endure, a few prisoners, although starving and suffering from extreme cold
themselves, would choose to comfort others and even
share their meager rations with weaker prisoners.

Frankl's conclusion was that the prisoners who survived chose an attitude of "What does life expect of me"
rather than "What do I expect from life." Frankl states that
we always have a choice. We may not be able to directly
change the circumstance, at least immediately, but we do
have the power to change attitude. Attitude comes from
the meaning we assign to events, people, substances, etc.
If we change meaning, we can change attitude. Seemingly
obvious, meaning is a function of thought.

One of the greatest abilities humans possess is the
ability to direct thought. It is our most creative act
because the world is shaped by ideas, images, and language. This even includes our bodies. If you hate yourself, which comes from an idea (thought) you have about
yourself, you will act in some "creative" ways to validate
the fact that you are right. You create a despicable,
worthless person because of the belief.[1] You might
express this hatred through violence toward others or
violence toward yourself. The violence may be brutal
and gross. Or it may be as subtle as smoking cigarettes.
The fact is that you cannot nurture something or someone you don't like, including yourself. You begin nurtur-

ing first by changing the thoughts and ideas your have about yourself . . . and the nurturing will spill over into nurturing others. Therefore, the self-improvement enterprise is not a selfish enterprise.

> The thought manifests as the word
> The word manifests as the deed
> The deed develops into habit
> And the habit hardens into character.
> So watch the thought
> And its ways with care
> And let it spring from love
> Born out of respect for all beings.
> —Dharma teaching, cited in
> Frances Vaughan, *The Inward Arc,* p. 15

It is thought that assigns meaning to the food, the event, or a choice. Constant suffering, feelings of desperation, misery, and self-pity inevitably set one up for failure. These negative feelings do not build character but rather sap one's energy. Fighting a battle is difficult if not impossible with such flagging energy. Take heart. Negative feelings can be supplanted with feelings of pride, increased self-esteem, and joy through the process of changing thought patterns. But it goes even further than that.

A perceptual shift or orientation needs to occur for meaning to change, and the tools to implement this change are imagination and language. The perceptual shift, or a different way to see the "world," is what makes positive choice natural and effortless. At first, it is a little like learning to swim . . . think about the kick, the pull, the head position while you quickly submerge to the bottom of the pool! Once you know how to swim, you dive in and swim to the end of the pool without a thought to the particulars of the stroke. You can enjoy.

You may have found that at one time or another you felt extremely resourceful and powerful. During this time, your energy created a sense of self-confidence accompanied by the feeling that you could accomplish virtually anything. Wouldn't it be grand to be able to summon up that mind-set and energy on command? How can we do it?

One can change mind-sets most effectively by shifting perception and focusing on varying aspects of a problem or situation. For example, this introduction began with abysmal statistics and failures. You can focus on the 95 per cent who fail. I purposely led you to focus on failure to make a point about diets. However, with practice, you can learn always to focus on success and opportunity no matter where someone else is trying to lead you. Therefore, you are in control.

The question that should have been itching for an answer is, "But what about the 5 per cent? I want to know about them. Some people make it." As Bernie Siegel points out in his book, *Love, Medicine, and Miracles*, you are not a statistic. You are a person. Statistics don't decide anything. People do. You do. "Statistical descriptions are pictures of crowd behavior. Statistics cannot tell us how one individual in a crowd will behave" (Zukav, 1979, p.33). Your decisions choose your future as well as your present.

Through mental strategies, you will become apart from the crowd behavior. You will see the world differently than the crowd does. You will have the ability to move with ease from one frame of reference to another. Thus, you will be able to make better decisions and make them with ease. You will "see" things that others cannot.

One of my clients, "Sally," had lunch with one of her friends at the country club. They both ordered a chef's salad. Sally used lemon juice instead of dressing, eliminated the egg yolk and some of the cheese, and ate unbuttered bread sticks.

As her friend gobbled up blue cheese dressing and other tasty morsels, she said, "Oh dear, you're taking all the good stuff off."

Sally replied, "No, I'm taking all the bad stuff off."

Sally's friend only knew food at the level of sight, smell, and taste. Sally also knew the food at the level of sight, smell, and taste, but she knew much more. She knew the level of cholesterol, saturated fat, salt, and calories. She knew want she wanted and valued and why her choices were important. She made a choice based on knowledge that her friend just did not have.

Sally's knowledge was not merely "head" knowledge. It was an integration of the head and heart . . . facts braided into desire and self-worth. Sally was not like Woody Allen when he stated in *Crimes and Misdemeanors*, "It's very hard to get your heart and head together in life. In my case, they're not even friendly." Sally will always "see" food differently than most people. It seems that, once perception has expanded, the awareness will always be there. You won't lose it like you did the formula for finding the area of a cylinder.

There are hundreds of examples of perceptual knowing. Birdwatchers see birds differently than I do. They see the species, the shape and color of the beak, the length of the feathers, the hue on the head and breast, etc. All I see is a robin. In the world of birds, the birdwatcher's life is much richer than mine. In the world of food and eating, my world is much richer with fruits and vegetables than some other people's are with cream and gravy. It is all a matter of learning. You will learn to enrich your life with gifts of awareness. Life becomes a joyful challenge instead of a series of never-ending battles. Whether it be the battle against fat or finances, life need not be a war.

Chances are that most of us, most of the time, just react and respond to stimuli in our environment. We never consider the fact that we have a choice about how we think about the stimuli. Belief, opinion, and attitude have become habitual. We are much like the computer which is programmed by past experience to "respond." The behavior is very predictable if you know the program. You can probably identify several of your own predictable behavior patterns related to food and circumstance. For example, you may avoid buying ice cream because, if you know it is in the freezer, you'll eat it. The "robot" is responding to the stimulus of knowing ice cream is in the freezer. Command: Eat it! Just a response. There is no creative thought in the process, therefore the response is always the same. No power. No control. No responsibility.

However, to be successful, you need power, control and responsibility. Together, we will discover ways to get back all these essential components of success. The fact is that you already have one of the three, power. You just may not realize it yet.

How do you tame the dragon? How will you get the power, control, and responsibility you need? The answer is through three primary mental strategies; namely, "languaging," imagining, and listening to the natural signals of your body. There are two primary ways in which we think. One is in words or language and the other is through the senses; i.e., in pictures, sounds, tactile and kinesthetic sensations, tastes, smells, and emotions. By creating thoughts, a type of energy, we influence body and emotional processes. Research supports this premise.

Your own experience will validate it later as you move through the activities in this book. The skills you will develop through practicing the exercises will enable you to create the outcome you wish. The combination of imagery and language creates the ultimate transformation of behavior toward life-affirming choices.

Imagery, the subject of Part I of this book, appears to be the quickest way to affect perception and physiology. The pioneers of biofeedback research, Elmer and Alyce Green of the Menninger Clinic, stated:

> Every change in the physiological state is accompanied by an appropriate change in the mental emotional state, conscious or unconscious, and conversely, every change in the mental emotional state, conscious or unconscious, is accompanied by an appropriate change in the physiological state.
>
> —Simonton, *et al.*, 1978, p. 29

My own research on the effects of guided imagery on basal metabolic rate [BMR], the number of calories burned at rest in 24 hours, produced remarkable results. Every one of the 57 participates significantly increased their BMRs within 11 minutes with only approximately 10 minutes of instruction (Kirk, 1988). You will have the benefit of more thorough instruction and practice.

Languaging, covered in Part II, is necessary to affect long-term changes in attitude, faith, and belief. Since there is an intimate interaction between imagery and languaging, we must work with both of them to be successful. Although we must deal with them one at a time, you will find that they are "braided" together.

Experiential Skills, Part III, is a separate section only because it does not fit nicely into the other categories. Life tends to be difficult to simplify! These experiential skills are useful in changing perception and gaining an appreciation for the marvelous organism that is your body. One focuses on awareness which is beyond words or images.

It does not matter which part you begin with, but keep in mind that they are all useful in some way. If you are eager to get to it, start with chapter 8, "The Personal Power Pack." It offers enough to get you started quickly and contains most of the information needed to understand the imagery and language. It was written in a self-contained form exactly for the purpose of a quick start. However, the other information is necessary to fully appreciate the value of the techniques as well as to develop the skills necessary to expand on the techniques on your own in a creative way.

You will find that you will prefer some techniques over others. Use what works. I encourage you to give all of them a chance. Practice each one of them several times before making final judgments.

This is a book to EXPERIENCE. It only works when you do. So find a special place to work that is comfortable and quiet where you will not be interrupted. Record your exercises in a journal. Avoid the temptation to shorten the process of the exercises by doing them "in your head" rather than on paper. Writing and drawing are essential elements of the process.

If you faithfully practice the techniques, I guarantee positive results. As you utilize these resources to discover your own resources, experiment with an open, receptive mind. The "beginner's mind" is the best indication of readiness for change. Play with and enjoy the exercises and knowledge you are about to experience. The only way the exercises can possibly work is for you to experience them. I am often asked about the success rate for this "program." Is it better than 5 per cent? I honestly do not know the statistic because it is so difficult to keep track of and follow clients over a long period of time. However, I have found repeatedly that clients were successful when they practiced their techniques consistently. Their progress appears to be directly proportional to the consistency of their practice.[2]

Perseverance is vitally important. Og Mandino beautifully expressed the metaphors of persistence,

> . . . I will be liken to the rain drop which washes away the mountain; the ant who devours a tiger; the star which brightens the earth; the slave who builds a pyramid.

An ant who happens to enjoy the taste of tiger meat might enjoy the prospect of having a whole tiger to himself. I understand that you may feel a bit more like the slave who has a pyramid to build rather than a hungry ant. I find the most amazing and encouraging aspects of human nature to be faith and hope. The fact that you have even started to read this book indicates a spark of that faith and hope. Together, we can ignite that faith into action of unbelievable strength and effect.

I invite and challenge you to make your first act in creating life-affirming thought a decision to accept this process as a joyful, exciting opportunity to learn. Embrace the adventure.

And now, sit down with your journal and begin.

Notes

1. People who have suffered any kind of abuse as children are likely to perceive themselves as powerless and unworthy especially if they were not allowed to express their feelings of anger, rage, or hurt. Tragically, as adults, they tend to become the abusers and perpetuate violence either toward themselves and/or others. These people are carrying awesomely heavy, destructive burdens into their adult lives. Abuse is the barrier blocking health and growth just as surely as Earl's brick blocked the growth of the seed. Ultimately, the abuse must be confronted and mourned as the first critical step toward the goal of leading a vital, happy life.

    I highly recommend Alice Miller's work, especially her book, *For Your Own Good* (1983), for those who have or suspect abuse in their childhood.

2. I want to know how you are doing and encourage you to write to me through the publisher. Sharing experiences, failures, frustrations, successes, and suggestions are valuable to me not only from a personal standpoint but from a professional one as well. Your experience may well influence the course of further research and refinements in techniques.

PART I

LANGUAGING

Those people who think they can do something
and those who think they can't are both right.
—Henry Ford

He who wants to keep his garden tidy, doesn't
reserve a plot for weeds.
—Dag Hammarskjold

•1•

Languaging: The Key to Unlocking Limitless Possibilities

Attention shapes the self, and is in turn shaped by it.

—*Mihaly Csikszentmihalyi*

In Csikszentmihalyi's wonderful work on the psychology of optimal experience (1990), he explains that the content of our consciousness can be ordered or disordered. The degree to which we feel fulfilled and happy depends upon the degree of our orderliness.

We experience order in consciousness when psychic or mind energy is invested in accomplishing worthwhile goals and when actions are congruent with one's value systems. Ordered consciousness means our attention is focused and we are free from worry, boredom, and self-doubt. Conversely, disorder of consciousness is experienced when psychic energy is depleted as a result of stimuli which draw attention away from our goals and value systems. Disorder of consciousness can be thought of as chaotic thoughts, the inability to maintain focus, erratic thoughts, and negative emotions such as fear, hate, resentment, etc. Disorder carries with it varying degrees of discomfort, pain, and suffering.

Csikszentmihalyi's work can easily be applied to the problem of weight control and/or eating disorders. Most everyone who has "dieted" has experienced disordered consciousness. For example, Helen has a goal of being 125 pounds instead of her current 180 pounds. Her goal is clear. She knows what she needs to do. However, her attention is constantly drawn to abundant negative food choices . . . the ads on television, the smell of burgers and fries from the Fast Food Strip on her way home from work, the cookies her children eat after school, ad infinitum. Her psychic energy is depleted further by her fear of the loss of control, loss of faith in herself, and self-denigrating statements when she slips up. Her disorder of consciousness creates a great deal of pain and suffering, saps her energy, and thwarts success. She is not happy when she diets, and chances are pretty good that her family isn't either.

The obvious question then is, "How do we get order?" Is order possible in a culture with so many temptations?

Order is possible, but it requires an investment of psychic energy. There is no need to be afraid of the investment because the fact is that you are continually investing psychic energy in some direction or another. The only way to NOT invest is to stop thinking. This does not even happen in sleep. Thought can be ordered or disordered, pleasant or unpleasant, joyful or miserable. The purpose of this entire work is to put the war to rest, which amounts to changing disorder to order. In essence, this is what transforms suffering into enjoyment.

Thoughts are a form of energy which may be creative and life-affirming or destructive and self-denigrating. The forms of thought are language and image. We think primarily in two ways—words and images (pictures, sounds, smells, etc.). We don't have much of a choice in term of producing thought energy. Thought happens. We do, however, have tremendous power in our ability to transform and direct thought. This most amazing gift is the hallmark of creativity, a birthright most of us do not know we have. It is a gift that most of us must work on to develop. Languaging will be one of the tools we use to order consciousness; imagination is the other, which will be addressed in Part II.

Transformation begins with the ability to direct attention *at will*. We all have the ability to switch attention. For example, direct your attention to the pressure of your body against the chair, feel the clothes against your skin, the sounds around you. Until you voluntarily shifted your attention, you probably were oblivious to these sensations. Note also that just by shifting attention you opened your perception . . . you see and hear parts of the world that were not there before. That is, they were not there only because they were not in your consciousness.

There is an insidious catch here. You did not direct your attention *at will*. You directed your attention because I suggested you focus on these stimuli. To direct attention *at will*, you must be the one to voluntarily focus on whatever you choose. Take a minute and do this. Focus on anything. Pretty easy. But is it? Now, choose one thing to focus on and maintain your focus for one minute. Only focus on this one thing of your choosing without thinking of anything else. Try it right now.

How many times and how many other things did you think about? As you see, it is relatively easy to shift attention at will, but it is extremely difficult to maintain focus even when there are no distractions. When you have chosen the object of attention, you are in effect using autosuggestion, meaning literally self-suggestion. The ability to focus on thoughts of your creation and intention is the true key to exercising "will" power.

Will power is not a "grit your teeth and bear it" capability. It is rather the ability to bring and focus your attention on your true values and goals. Will power is evidence of ordered consciousness rather than evidence of self-inflicted denial. When you are focused on your true wants and needs rather than on conflicting suggestions, it is easy to act in consistent ways. The action is easy when there is focus. The focus is the difficult thing to maintain. In Eastern philosophy the mind is sometimes referred to as a drunken monkey. Disciplining the mind is like training a drunken monkey—a bit of a challenge.

Will power would not be such a difficult thing to exercise if we could eliminate the ubiquitous nature of the suggestion of others. From the very moment we are born, we are infused with suggestions as to how we should act, what we should be, how we should perform, what we should want. The suggestions become internalized to the point that even distinguishing between what we truly need and want from what others want from us is a confusing and difficult task.

Our culture suggests strongly that we should be fit and trim . . . more trim than fit. Our culture rewards fit and trim but does not reward the *process of getting* fit and trim. In a magazine, there is an article on how to get thinner thighs in 30 days and a double chocolate fudge cake recipe on the opposite page. "You deserve a break today." "Aren't you hungry right now?" And so on. Smokers and drinkers are surrounded by friends in a natural setting or at a party, not at a hospital or grave site. That is just advertising. "If you get any thinner, you'll blow away." "You just *have* to have a piece of cake." "Your brother doesn't do that." "Why aren't you more like so-and-so?" "Your mother and father were both heavy." "All the women in the family are fat."

All of these are suggestions—some through language, some through images. If you do nothing to consciously process the content and the effects of the content on your consciousness, you may own these suggestions. They become part of your reality without any voluntary control. The suggestions are programmed into your brain, and the program will trigger its own repetition in the form of self-talk.

Every time the message is repeated it is reinforced and becomes stronger and more powerful.

You are being manipulated for the benefit of the bottom line, be it money, security, or whatever. If you are conscious, you can decide if you want the suggestion to be your reality. Some suggestion is so subtle or even subliminal that you may not get to decide. But with training and alertness, you will begin to recognize much of it as blatant and ridiculous. Some will be easy to discard. Some will be positive and you will welcome them. The point is that this is the beginning of self-control. We only have limited control of our environment, but we can choose to create positive thought energy. This is the ultimate in control because what we think generates our feelings and perceptions.

Much of the literature on self-talk and auto-suggestion states that people can "reprogram" their self-talk, as if the old suggestions were somehow eliminated through this reprogramming. I don't happen to believe this. We can certainly change our habitual thinking patterns, but over and over again I have seen the old patterns reappear.

This reappearance happens when one is under stressful circumstances. For example, John has been working two jobs so he can afford to pay his weight-loss counselor, his car just died, and his insurance is past due. All of a sudden, despite the fact that he has been progressing well on his program, he "unhinges his jaw and eats the refrigerator." The old program of eating for comfort and sedation arise again. To insure the old program remains dormant, one must make the new program stronger than the old one or we must effectively manage the stress in our lives. We will examine several ways to do this.

The first step in strengthening will power and gaining self-control is to recognize suggestion pointblank and to ask, "What is the objective or the real message of the suggestion?" Ideally, we want to recognize the irrationality, self-deceit, mistaken assumptions, or manipulation contained in suggestions emanating from both inside and outside ourselves. Once we recognize the message, then we will attempt to change it to its accurate message.

Any time negative language is changed to positive language for the purpose of suggestion, you are tapping into a subtle but extremely powerful mode of transformation. Language can change your beliefs, expectations, attitudes, knowledge, and perception, which in turn change your life profoundly. Through autosuggestion, you can transform yourself into your own creative, life-affirming ideal. You can become the winner, the champion you deserve to be. And, through increasingly ordered consciousness and wise investment of psychic energy, you will have fun doing it. There are many tools of language with which to accomplish this.

I have taken liberty of entitling this part "Languaging" rather than "Language" because I would like you to think of this process as a verb . . . language as action. So, here we go.

Recognizing, Interpreting, and Transforming Negative Language

Start listening to people and yourself speak. Become acutely aware of what it is that people are really saying. Language gives clues and insights into how people think, how they impose limits upon themselves, how they give themselves escape routes from responsibility, or their willingness to accept responsibility, commitment, personal power, and freedom. It can tell us if one sees the world optimistically or pessimistically.

Becoming aware of language is the first step to changing the way you think. The exercises on the following pages will help you do this.

EXERCISE ONE

Analyze common statements. The following are examples of some very common statements people have made. You have, no doubt, either heard similar comments or uttered them yourself at one time or another. The task is to interpret the comments. Are they positive, negative, or realistic? *Positive* **means that the comment promotes life and liveliness;** *negative* **means the statement destroys, nullifies, or in some way degrades life and spirit.** Ask yourself, "Is the comment limiting potential and growth?" Is it a rationalization; i.e., a self-deception? Self-deception is a lie and cannot promote life and liveliness. Does it imply or assume expectation? Record your interpretation of the comments in your journal. Then change the comments that are negative to positive statements. Pay particular attention to comments that imply expectation of behavior or performance.

Note that the comments are not restricted to weight control or eating issues. We must be more global and all-inclusive in order to influence habitual thought patterns. People who are negative in one area of their lives tend to be negative in other areas.

Refer to Appendix A for interpretations. My interpretations are by no means the only interpretations. If you come up with others, they may be just as valid.

A. "I am going to try to lose 10 pounds by Christmas."

B. "Just my luck. They'll probably be out of my size by the time we get there."

C. "You just have to try the cherry pie! It's delicious."

Continued →

Exercise One—Cont'd.

D. " I'll just die if I can't make the team."

E. Question: "How are you today?" Answer: "Not too bad."

F. "You think that's bad. Wait 'til you hear about what happened to me!"

G. Today's forecast: Partly cloudy with occasional snow flurries.

H. "I am going to quit drinking alcohol, totally, until I lose 20 pounds."

I. "I am going to start my diet right after the holidays."

J. "My parents always made us clean our plates. We were brought up to 'waste not, want not.'"

K. "Lordy! I'm stuffed but this is so-o-o good. Just a few more bites."

L. "I'm big-boned."

M. "My husband won't let me work."

N. "I grew up with a German grandma and you know German food."

O. "Isn't it just awful about Mildred, poor thing?"

P. "You didn't actually expect to get that job, did you?"

Q. "All the questions on the math test tomorrow are going to be word problems. I just hate word problems. I'm not good at them."

R. "I'll probably screw it up. I always do."

S. "What'd you expect?"

EXERCISE TWO

Write it down. Carry a small notebook around with you for several days and write down comments you hear others voicing, or thoughts you voice or think which you interpret as either positive or negative. Change all negative statements and thoughts to positive ones. The purpose of this exercise and the previous one is to increase your awareness and to initiate changing your own thought patterns to growth-promoting ones. At this point, *it is extremely important* that you write the comments down along with their changes. Writing will force precision in thought. It is too easy to be sloppy and careless with merely thinking interpretation and changes. Of course, the ultimate objective is to make a habit of growth-promoting thought. When this is accomplished, writing can be eliminated. We behave in growth-promoting ways only if we think in growth-promoting ways. If we think negatively, we will produce negative results. Thinking positively will also prevent us from falling victim to other people's negativity and deception.

EXERCISE THREE

Watch a soap opera. Soaps are veritable smorgasbords of negativity flavored with guilt, blame, misplaced guilt and blame, lack of responsibility, and lessons in non-communication. As a matter of fact, most network programming is negative, and a continual diet of such fare is not healthy. However, the purpose of this exercise is to increase your awareness and, as such, the capability of protecting yourself from negativity. With a little practice, you will find yourself interpreting all situations automatically. Negative statements will seem to quite literally jump out at you.

Record specific examples of dialogue which reflect disorder of consciousness. How could the character change? Think precisely, particularly when changing or adding to possibilities. You will discover that, if all soap characters reflected ordered consciousness, there would no longer be a story line in the true sense of the morality play.

EXERCISE FOUR

Eavesdrop . . . with a modicum of discretion, of course.

Listen to other people's conversations in restaurants, locker rooms, or any place where it is nearly impossible *not* to eavesdrop anyway.

Interpret. Change. WRITE IT DOWN!

EXERCISE FIVE

Observe the media. Watch the news and television commercials, read the newspaper and newspaper advertising. Interpret and practice changing negatives to positives whenever possible. You will find this exercise challenging, especially if you try it for the first five pages of the newspaper.

Take the time to invest in these exercises and be certain to refer to Appendix A. If you discovered that you automatically think negatively, do not be discouraged. As you have no doubt discovered , we are surrounded with negativity. Negativity is the norm. You have become aware of the problem and that is a quantum leap toward personal transformation. The ability to order consciousness, to be positive regardless of the circumstances is an attribute of a champion. You are taking the first steps toward the development of that ability through the use of these exercises.

Transformation Through Autosuggestion

Remember, to order consciousness we need to invest our psychic energy in accomplishing worthwhile goals and to act in ways which are consistent with our goals and values. To do this effectively we must discipline our minds to focus on suggestions which will generate the energy we need to act in ways which fulfill our desires. Since negativity is the norm, it is virtually impossible to acquire the energy of positive suggestion from our culture. Therefore, we must create it ourselves. Of course, we do that by focusing our attention on our own creative thoughts. We may also establish "Master Mind" groups, which are small groups of people which foster and create positive, energizing collective thought . . . a kind of support group brought together to help each other fulfill potential rather than share a specific problem. The "Master Mind" concept will be addressed later.

> Autosuggestion is a term which applies to all suggestions and all self-administered stimuli which reach one's mind through the five senses . . . self-suggestion. It is the agency of communication between the part of the mind where conscious thought takes place, and that which serves as the seat of action for the subconscious mind.
>
> Through the dominating thoughts which one permits to remain in the conscious mind (whether these thoughts be negative or positive is immaterial), the principle of autosuggestion voluntarily reaches the subconscious mind and influences it with these thoughts.
>
> —Hill, 1960, p. 67

There are many ways to influence the mind with autosuggestion. "But what thoughts will create the action

I need to result in the transformation I desire? And how do I use them; how do I actually program my mind?" Well, if we become experts at identifying negative thoughts and changing them on the spot, that might be enough. From what we know to date, it seems that repetition is necessary and that the message can be effectively delivered to the conscious and subconscious mind in a variety of ways. Delivery varies, but the positive suggestion is an affirmation. The message itself depends upon one's goals, needs, values, beliefs, and expectations. Therefore, it is evident that different people need different affirmations and the same person may need different affirmations at different times. Thus self-knowledge is vital in discovering and creating the affirmation you need. The affirmations then become the objects of thought which create order in consciousness. They become the dominating thoughts which will yield the dominating action. You may find for the first time that "right" action becomes easy.

Suggested Reading:

Csikszentmihalyi, Mihaly. *Flow: The Psychology of Optimal Experience.* New York: Harper & Row, 1990.

Davis, Martha et al. *The Relaxation & Stress Reduction Workbook.* Oakland, CA: New Harbinger Publications, 1988. (Chapters 9 and 10).

· 2 ·

Designer Affirmations: Creating Your Own Growth Language

You have taken a giant leap in progress when you have developed your ability to identify and cognitively transform negative language to positive language. This is the beginning of the end of the struggle, for these changes yield changes in perception. Further, when one creates positive thought energy, one is also creating the momentum needed to easily actualize goals with a sense of challenge and adventure. There is an aura of excitement and enthusiasm surrounding the process of obtaining the goal instead of just having the goal. Work becomes play.

As pointed out previously, everyone needs different affirmations because of individual uniqueness. There are several effective ways of identifying personal affirmations which we will explore in this chapter. Then, the specifics of effective writing and use of affirmations will be discussed.

Pathways for Identifying Personal Affirmations

PATHWAY ONE

"That one is for me." The most obvious and most frequently used technique for identification is just to use the ones which someone else has identified but which seem to jump out at you as if they were written precisely with you in mind. This is certainly effective because the fact that you immediately identify with the statement means that it is needed and/or desired.

If you wish to get started right away, this is the way to begin. Refer to the "The Personal Power Pack," reading through the affirmations, and use any that trigger a pleasant, energetic response.

PATHWAY TWO

"The Ultimate Judgment." This pathway is one of my favorites because it is "global." That is, it helps to change one's habitual ways of thinking without regard to a specific problem. Although specifics are extremely important for solving problems, I believe it is absolutely necessary to change generally negative thought patterns to generally positive ones if the goal is realizing one's potential. As a health educator, that is always my foremost goal. Whether that is your goal is not necessarily important because the effect will be to move you toward your goal anyway, whatever it is. A weight or body-composition goal is specific, but the solution requires a solid foundation of positive belief, expectation, and commitment. The "Ultimate Judgment" builds the foundation.

This technique is borrowed from the ideas of Leonard Orr and his reference, the Buddha. Sit down with your journal in a quiet place where you will not be interrupted for an hour. Write down anything that comes to mind for 30-45 minutes. You will find that you think much faster than you can write. Therefore, you only need to write down words or phrases that capture the idea or image of your thought. This will be enough for you to be able to identify the complete thought later. This is an exercise for the drunken monkey . . . let the mind run amuck! There is no need to attempt to focus on any particular thought. This is not like writing a letter. There is no theme. Surrender and let the thought energy go without direction.

When you are finished writing, go back and

Continued →

Pathway Two—cont'd.

underline the negative statements or images. Remember, "negative" means that it destroys, nullifies, or in some way degrades life and spirit. Then, using your life-generating creativity, redesign the statements, transforming the negative to positive. This is a creative act and may take some time to juggle the elements of language. You might ask yourself, "What other meaning might I choose to assign to this thought, this event or feeling?" Take another perspective to get a different meaning. As a hiker the statement is, "Darn! The storm is going to ruin our trip up the pass." As a farmer, "Thank God! The storm will bring the rain we need for the corn crop." From the perspective of the greatest good for the greatest number, a corn crop is more important than a hike up the pass. And, from that perspective, there is no need to feel badly. In effect, the positive statement you have created is an affirmation. Therefore, you have designed your own affirmation. These affirmations are powerful for you because they are based upon your own thoughts, which express personal needs, feelings, desires, etc.

How did you feel while you were writing? How did your feelings change during the process of changing negative thoughts to affirmations?

Several things happen with this technique. One, writing serves to externalize negative emotion, which makes you feel better whether or not you develop your own affirmations. This means that it is a pretty good stress-management technique in and of itself.

Continued →

Pathway Two—cont'd.

Two, one may discover what Leonard Orr calls personal laws. Personal laws are beliefs we hold which define our self-concepts, our place in the world, the meanings we give to our lives, etc. These laws are laws primarily because we believe them. They may be based upon erroneous assumptions and adopted because we accepted them as true when we were children. Identifying personal laws again will allow us to decide if they are valid, if we wish to still act on them, or if we wish to create different, more life-affirming laws. Many times when we examine these laws rationally, they just do not make sense. Or, although they were valid at one time, they are now obsolete.

The example of the hiker's thought is not a personal law. The thought is an expression of disappointment or inconvenience. But we have a personal law if the hiker's thought was something like, "A storm. Every time I plan something I really look forward to, the rug is pulled out from under me." This is an expression of the belief that he better not look forward to anything because just looking forward to it will jinx the outcome. Is God or nature out to get him? Was he born a loser? It is the hiker who would most likely come up with the accurate interpretation of the statement. It requires personal reflection. You are the one to identify your own personal laws.

There may be faster ways to identify personal laws. One would probably need to do the Ultimate

Continued →

Pathway Two—cont'd.

Judgment many, many times to identify all of one's personal laws.

Three, thoughts become "objective." One becomes an observer of the thoughts and, to an observer, the thoughts lose some of their power. It is as if the thoughts are separate from the thinker and this separateness disconnects the effect produced by the thought. This is difficult to understand without experiencing it.

One winter night as I was driving home from my three-hour evening class, I became aware of the quality of my thoughts. Nearly all of my thoughts were expressions of anger and frustration . . . I hate serving on that committee; what a waste of precious time; my students can't spell worth a d#*&! . . . and so on. There were an unusually high number of expletives coming from a person who does not swear much!

Awareness of the content of the thought allowed me to become an observer of the thought. I was very tired and knew content was a function of fatigue, a universal stressor. I knew the thoughts were negative and unproductive, but I was too tired to deal with changing them. However, once I became the observer, the thoughts had no power. I didn't feel badly because of the thoughts but because of fatigue. Had I not become the observer, the thoughts would have made me feel worse.

Here is a short two minute example of the Ultimate Judgment.

First, write thoughts:

Continued →

Pathway Two—cont'd.

Hot in here; humid; wish she'd turn on the fan. I'm hungry. I'm fat. Pizza for lunch? Hope Bob doesn't show...ugh! Too many hours. Sharon in the office Smiling. Happy. Confident. I'm happy too. Will mom call? Is she okay? The doctor is a jerk. Fear, fear, nightmares.

Second, underline negatives:

Hot in here; humid; <u>wish she'd turn on the fan.</u> I'm hungry. I'm fat. Pizza for lunch? <u>Hope Bob doesn't show...ugh! Too many hours.</u> Sharon in the office. Smiling. Happy. Confident. I'm happy too. Will mom call? Is she okay? <u>The doctor is a jerk. Fear, fear, nightmares.</u>

Third, change negatives to positives:

I'll ask her to turn on the fan (do it); I am uncomfortable with Bob so I'll just avoid him and enjoy the other people at the party; I'm getting paid overtime, yippee!; The doctor is incompetent and I'll see if mom will consider getting another opinion; dreams are valuable messages . . . what do I have to learn?

Fourth, are there expressions of personal laws here? I don't think so, but let us explore. Do I need to work on expressing my needs and concerns? Do I need to ask the teacher to turn on the fan, ask my boss to decrease my hours, tell Bob I am not interested in him, talk with the doctor to understand her point of view, express my fears to mom, tell her that I love her? Here the writer would need to interpret because communication and assertiveness may or may not be a problem. I just do not know this unless I am the writer. You must work to interpret your own writing.

PATHWAY THREE

Mind-mapping is also called semantic webbing or clustering. It is used for a variety of purposes, but we will use it here for identifying specifics. The specifics are, namely, old messages which act as barriers to success, negative personal laws, and inhibiting suggestions from others which became internalized and therefore, our own. The barrier messages will be changed to positive autosuggestions and used in the form of affirmations.

Mind-mapping can be thought of as a kind of free association. We usually think of free association in terms of a one-word response triggered by another one-word stimulus. Stimulus: "Father" Response: "Mother." With mind-mapping, we free-associate until we run dry. The stimulus word, the kernel or nuclear word, is written in the center of the page and circled. This nuclear word is a multiordinate word in that it elicits many different images and meanings from different people. For example, if the nuclear word is "rose," one person may envision a bunch of red roses, another a single red rose, another yellow roses, another a wild rose in a garden, etc. One simple word generates as many different images and meanings as there are people. Individual uniqueness. Likewise, the images and meanings elicit many different feelings depending upon the associations or connections. *Rose*—funeral —grief; *Rose*—girlfriend—love—passion; *Rose*—mother—love—comfort—security, etc. From the central nuclear word, any freely associated word or image is attached by means of a line or spoke. See figure A. When one

Continued →

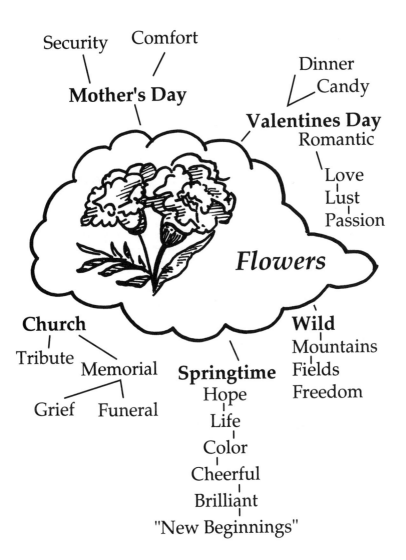

Security   Comfort

Mother's Day

Dinner
Candy

Valentines Day
Romantic

Love
Lust
Passion

Flowers

Church
Tribute
Memorial

Grief   Funeral

Springtime
Hope
Life
Color
Cheerful
Brilliant
"New Beginnings"

Wild
Mountains
Fields
Freedom

Figure A

Pathway Three—cont'd.

line of association is completed (words and images stop flooding the mind), go back to the nuclear word and freely associate creating another flow of thought.

The mapping is done quickly, effortlessly, and without judgment. It only takes about two to five minutes to complete. Speed of discovery is one its main advantages. Specificity is another . . . we can focus on particular problems.

The first examples (Figures A and B) are nouns chosen arbitrarily to demonstrate the technique. Upon examination, you will find that these arbitrary, seemingly meaningless words hold a great deal of meaning. The associations reveal factual knowledge and also feeling. They reveal meaning based on experience and circumstance, which, of course, is dependent upon the unique combination of learning and experiences of the individual. Because associations are so personal, if will be impossible for you to determine the quality of all the spokes. You will only be able to do this for your own mind-maps. However, some qualities are obvious. Refer to Figure A, "Flowers." The quality of the spoke starting with the word "church" might be negative . . . one does not feel good while grieving at a funeral. There is a great sense of personal loss. The quality of the spoke beginning with "springtime" is entirely different. Hope is an energizing emotion. You will notice that *all* of the examples have positive, negative, and neutral associations. Take a moment and try to identify the quality (positive, negative, or neutral) of the spokes in the

Continued →

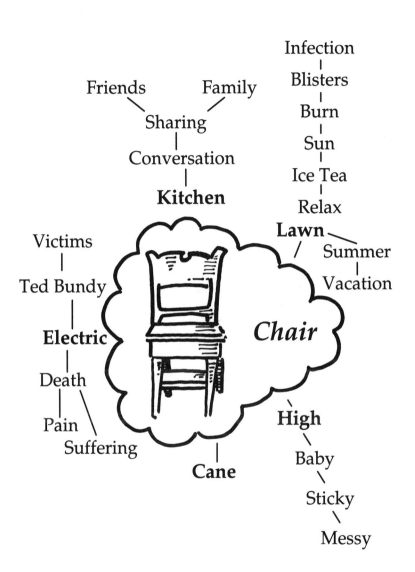

Friends — Family
Sharing
Conversation
Kitchen

Infection
Blisters
Burn
Sun
Ice Tea
Relax
Lawn
Summer
Vacation

Victims
Ted Bundy
Electric
Death
Pain
Suffering

Chair

High
Baby
Sticky
Messy

Cane

Figure B

Pathway Three—cont'd.

examples of Flowers (Figure A) and Chair (Figure B).

Just the vast number of associations may help explain why one may feel hopeful, energized, and excited about a goal one minute and plummet into feelings of despair, hopelessness, and defeat at another moment. The feeling is activated by the association. The specific association may be triggered by a wide variety of stimuli . . . a smell of a rose may trigger the association of comfort if I am in the garden at home. Or it may trigger a sense of loss if I smell the rose while walking past a cemetery.

We want to build stronger positive associations with existing connections and to create brand new ones if necessary. Affirmations allow us do this consciously and systematically.

Now we can discover knowledge, feelings, belief, etc. related to specifics and from this develop auto-suggestions. First, choose any two nouns to mind-map just for fun and practice. Do this in your journal. Second, mind-map the following as nuclear words. Only take two to five minutes to map each term.

Words to mind-map:

1. Your favorite food—which you think you should NOT have while on a diet. The nuclear word is the name of the food; e.g., "Ice Cream."

2. My Body

3. Exercise

4. Eating

5. Diet

6. Commitment

Continued →

Pathway Three—cont'd.

See Figures C through H for examples.

Now, go back and check the associations which hold a negative connotation. Just as you did with the Ultimate Judgment, write an affirmation to counter the negative. Before you do that, however, look at Figure C, Ice Cream, a favorite food (number one in the exercise). You will notice that most of the associations are positive: summer, fun, refreshing, cold, smooth, sweet. Even the spoke which began with a negative, a tonsillectomy, had many more positives than negatives: treat, reward, comfort, games, laughter, fun. Because of the strong positive association, I will naturally feel pretty good about ice cream (this is my mind-map, by the way). As a matter of fact, when I think of ice cream or am in some way triggered by the need for comfort or a treat, I have a very high probability of craving ice cream. But there is a conflict here if I want to lose weight or avoid heart disease, because ice cream has too much fat to be considered a good food choice. Therefore, to achieve my goal of weight loss, it is best to eliminate ice cream. Now here is where we can feel the strength of the associations because, when I say to myself, "I will not eat ice cream," I feel a little scared and even experience some psychic pain. Why? I am not just giving up a frozen dairy dessert when I give up ice cream. I am also giving up all my associations . . . the comfort, reward, fun, laughter, etc. That is why a diet may elicit intense feelings of desperation and why people are so totally miserable. It makes sense at the "gut-

Continued →

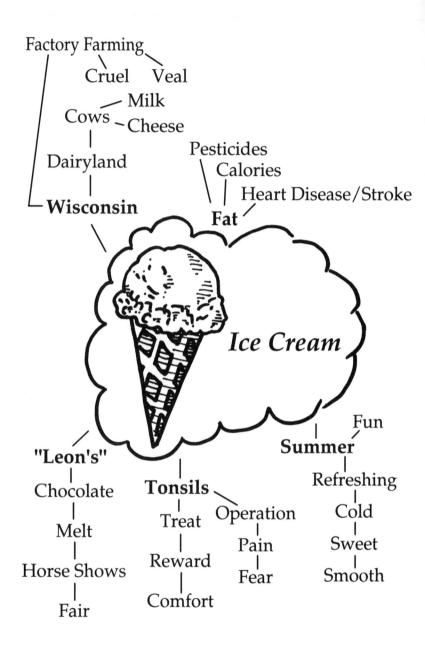

Factory Farming
Cruel   Veal
Milk
Cows — Cheese
Dairyland
Wisconsin

Pesticides
Calories
Heart Disease/Stroke
Fat

Ice Cream

"Leon's"
Chocolate
Melt
Horse Shows
Fair

Tonsils
Treat   Operation
Reward   Pain
Comfort   Fear

Summer   Fun
Refreshing
Cold
Sweet
Smooth

Figure C

Pathway Three—cont'd.

emotional feeling" level while making no sense at all at the rational level.

To eradicate these feelings of despair and misery, I have several choices. One, any time I see or think about ice cream, I can focus on the negative . . . too fat, heart disease, stroke, a barrier to my goal, which is much more important the temporary sensory gratification, etc. We will work much more with this in the imagery section.

Two, I can shift my focus and think of something else. When I think ice cream, I want ice cream. I cannot "not think," but I can easily shift attention and gain ordered consciousness. Remember, to have ordered consciousness and be happy, my actions must be congruent with my goals. I violate my goal if I eat ice cream, creating my own disorder and unhappiness. I chose to think my goal and why it is important. Therefore, my goal statement is an affirmation, "I will be 112 pounds by September 2."

Three, I can substitute another product for ice cream; e.g., low-fat frozen yogurt, and through new experiences build new and strong associations. The associations built on acting on the best choices are feelings of success, self-confidence, and respect.

Four, I can find more appropriate ways to reward myself and gain comfort. Speaking strictly in terms of affirmations, the goal statement is the most effective for "ice cream." But can we come up with others?

Continued →

Pathway Three—cont'd.

Examples:

1. "Good food choices are gifts to myself." Notice, the object of thought is no longer ice cream. The object will become whatever the good food choices are, be it frozen yogurt or green beans.

2. "I make good choices easily and effortlessly."

3. "I love and respect my body."

4. "Every time I make good food choices, I am making all of the cells and systems of my body stronger, healthier, and more alive."

Lastly, identify personal laws that may need to be changed. This example, Ice Cream, does not express any personal laws. There may be laws revealed in this type of example, however. It may be that one believes it impossible to trust others and can therefore only get comfort and reward from food. Food is safe; people are dangerous. A person with this belief must find more appropriate ways to get comfort and reward or he will never be successful with weight/eating control goals. Weight/eating problems are multidimensional, which is why no one solution or affirmation works for everyone.

Look through the examples and see if you can find associations which may reflect personal laws. Do not be afraid to venture some guesses. Play with ideas. This is fun to work on with someone else.

Refer to Figure D-1 and D-2. Can you distinguish differences in personal laws? D-1 was done by someone who has a pretty good self-concept. She likes, enjoys, and values her body but becomes a

Continued →

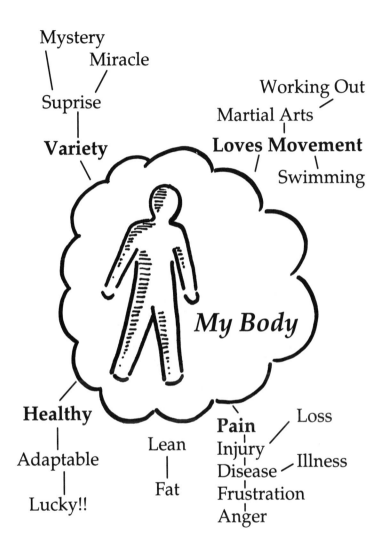

Figure D-1

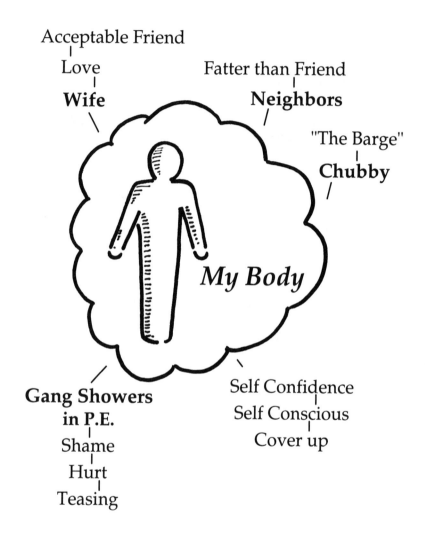

Acceptable Friend
Love
Wife

Fatter than Friend
Neighbors

"The Barge"
Chubby

My Body

**Gang Showers
in P.E.**
Shame
Hurt
Teasing

Self Confidence
Self Conscious
Cover up

Figure D-2

Pathway Three—cont'd.

little angry and frustrated when the body breaks down momentarily. She perceives her body as much as a mystery and a miracle as it is a gift. One would guess that she nourishes her body well because of her love and respect for it. She will only need affirmations during times when the body is in distress. When she is sick or injured, appropriate affirmations would include: "Health is my natural state of being." "My body heals quickly and easily." "I listen and learn from the lessons my body teaches me." She has some healthy personal laws because they are life-affirming.

Contrast person D-1 with person D-2. Again, we are playing with ideas. One of his personal laws is imprinted in his identity. He was teased and hurt. His identity is one of a rejected, obese person. Luckily, he found acceptance and love with a wife who is his friend. Self-love and self-like are necessary to grow and express potential. You cannot nurture something you do not like. He needs and may have, in fact, accepted himself where he is, which will allow him to progress further. If not, he may use affirmations such as: "I love myself completely." "I have a valuable contribution to make." "I love and respect my body." "I love and respect myself." "I deserve to be successful." "I am ready and willing to accept love and success into my life." "God wants me to succeed." There are many others. His personal laws must reflect self-worth.

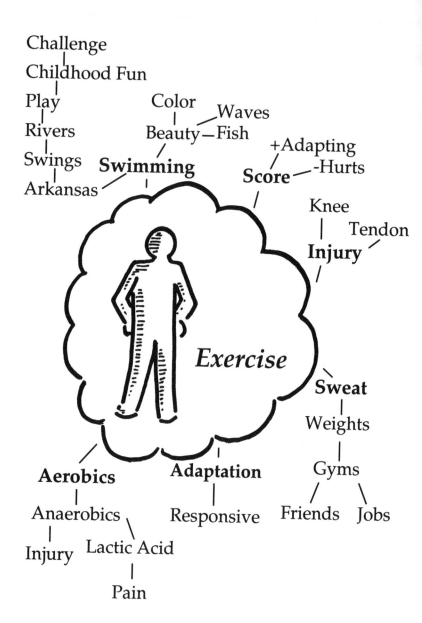

Figure E

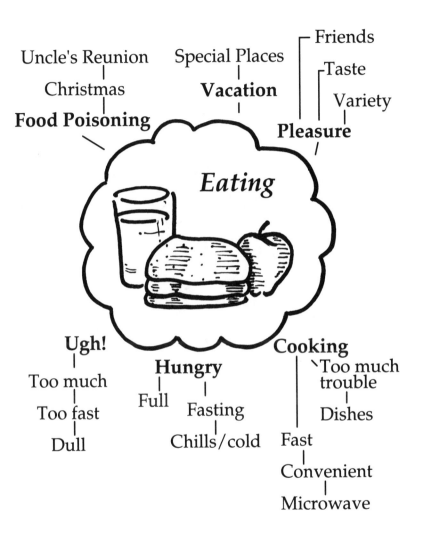

Figure F

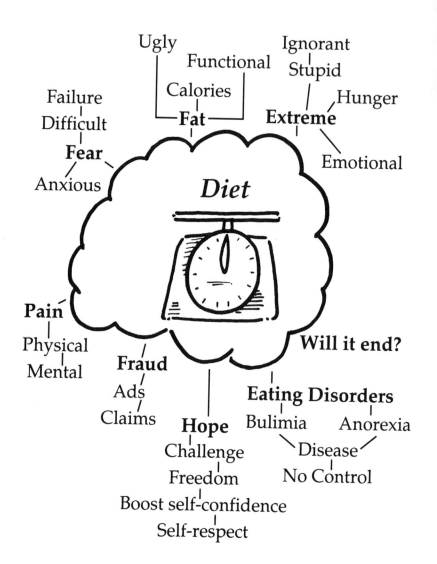

Ugly
Functional
Ignorant
Stupid
Hunger
Failure
Calories
Extreme
Difficult
Fat
Fear
Emotional
Anxious

Diet

Pain
Physical
Mental
Will it end?

Fraud
Ads
Claims
Eating Disorders
Bulimia
Anorexia
Hope
Challenge
Disease
Freedom
No Control
Boost self-confidence
Self-respect

Figure G

Figure H

PATHWAY FOUR

Characteristics of Successful/Admired People. In your journal, write down the names of three people you admire and/or three people you believe are "successful." Then write down the characteristics these people have which you think make them successful or admirable. Another variation of this is to list the characteristics a person would need to achieve your goals. Add these characteristics to your list. Then, develop affirmations from those characteristics which you want and need to strengthen.

Example

Admired people: Martin Luther King, Jr., Aunt Nellie, Mrs. Johnson (7th grade teacher)

Characteristics: Had a vision, courageous, strong faith, personal integrity, sense of humor, tenacious, assertive, persistent, intelligent, respectful, honest, disciplined

Successful people: Woody Allen, Golda Meir, Mohandas Gandhi, Pablo Picasso, Uncle Don

Characteristics: Creative, worked to develop and express talent, focused, loved their work, had fun working, sense of humor, personal integrity, honest, disciplined, vision, courageous, ability to overcome adversity, mental and physical consistency.

Characteristics needed to achieve my goal:

Tenacity, persistence, will power, consistency, a vision, personal integrity, faith, courage, discipline, commitment, enthusiasm.

Continued →

Pathway Four—cont'd.

From this list, I can generate many affirmations but I will first focus on the ones where I am weakest.

Examples

"I have and exercise the power I have to create my own life."

"I now easily and naturally use all my resources to succeed."

"I accept life as an opportunity to learn and grow."

"Failure is an opportunity to learn."

"I have the strength and creativity to change adversity into opportunity."

And so on...

Notice how these affirmations function to change perception. At one time, failure may have meant defeat. Now it is on opportunity to learn. The first meaning of failure puts one in a helpless-hopeless state, which is one of the most dangerous and unresourceful states of mind one can be in. The second meaning totally diffuses failure's negative connotation. Well, this way did not work. What other ways are there to succeed? This meaning challenges one's creative abilities, and through that challenge one grows and becomes a more complex, interesting individual.

PATHWAY FIVE

Countering Barriers to Success. List all the reasons why you think you cannot achieve your goal. Then write affirmations to counter the barriers.

Example: "I will be 120 pounds by September 2."

Not enough time. There are a lot of birthdays and parties coming up and I always pig out. I should wait to start on this. What will my family eat while I'm on a diet? I don't want to have to fix two meals, one for me and one for my family.

Affirmations

"I can achieve anything I set my mind to."

"I am responsible for my own needs. Others are responsible for their needs."

"We all have the same amount of time. I choose to use my time to create the life and body I want."

"I naturally make good food choices."

"Good choices are easy to make."

And so on...

You can literally generate thousands of personal affirmations via these four pathways. Unfortunately, it is impractical to work with hundreds at a time. Nevertheless, go ahead and generate as many as possible without reservation. You will know intuitively which ones are most important.

Rules for Writing Affirmations

The rules for writing affirmations are simple but easily overlooked. After you have written several affirmations, check the rules to make sure they are in the proper, most effective form.

1. The statement is *totally* positive. Exclude words such as try, not, cannot, will not, should not, ought not.

Correct: "I will be 120 pounds by September 2."
Incorrect: "I will try to lose 10 pounds by September 2.

Correct: "I make positive food choices."
Incorrect: "I will not eat ice cream."

2. The statement is in the present tense whenever possible.

Correct: "I am now creating my life just as I want it."
Incorrect: "I will go to graduate school if I get a divorce."

Correct: "I deserve to be successful."
Incorrect: "I will make more money if I get the job promotion."
Incorrect: "I will be successful if I can get an education."

3. Make the statement as close to believable as possible. If you hate to exercise...

Correct: "I love the effects of exercise."
Incorrect: "I love to exercise."

The believable form may be enough to get you to exercise and, after you are in good physical condition, then the "I love to exercise" may be believable enough to use.

Application of Affirmations

Now that you have all these wonderful affirmations, what do you do with them? How do we get them to work? Refer to "The Personal Power Pack" for specifics. The following is a brief summary.

1. Choose 3 - 5 to work with the first week.

2. Write each one on a note card and read through them three times per day and before situations which may be difficult to get through successfully. Read them right before going to sleep.

3. Write each affirmation 10 to 20 times in first, second and third person. Write down any negative response you have to the affirmation for the first three or four times. You may then just ignore the negatives, or the negatives may generate other needed affirmations. Example: "I deserve to be successful . . . but my Daddy said I'd never be worth a damn." New affirmation: "I forgive my father completely."

For about two years, I started each day with writing 20 to 28 affirmations. Usually, it did wonders for setting the tone of the day. However, there was a period of time I just could not stand to do them, although I was not sure why. I normally enjoyed this special beginning of the day. Out of frustration, I turned to my journal and let the anger and frustration pour out onto the pages. These feelings were blocking any attempts at positive suggestion and needed to be acknowledged. Once the feelings were expressed, acknowledged, and accepted as part of the process of growth, I discovered I could go back to work with the affirmations again. Perhaps more importantly, I discovered the source of the anger and frustration so that I could deal with it directly instead of feeling badly.

4. Change affirmations as needed.

An important note: You are not truly finished with an affirmation until it is totally integrated into your consciousness—waking and otherwise. The old triggers should consistently elicit the new thought rather than the old habitual message, or, as soon as the old message is voiced, it is immediately identified as such and replaced easily with the affirmation. I think the biggest mistake people make with the use of affirmations is that they stop using them prematurely . . . stopping short is like aborting a day-old fetus. It is not strong enough to survive because it isn't mature. It never had a chance to survive. The only way an affirmation matures is through the nurturing by repetition.

5. Tape the affirmation and goals. This will be discussed later.

Suggested Reading:

Burns, David. *Feeling Good: The New Mood Therapy.* New York: Signet, 1980.

Coué, Emile and Brooks, C.H. *Self Mastery through Conscious Auto-Suggestion: The Practice of Autosuggestion by the Method of Emile Coué.* Winchester, MA: Allen & Unwin, 1984.

Gawain, Shakti. *Reflections in the Light, Daily Thoughts and Affirmations.* San Rafael, CA: New World Library, 1988.

Hill, Napoleon. *Think and Grow Rich.* New York: Fawcett Crest Books, 1960.

Maltz, Maxwell. *Psycho-Cybernetics.* New York: Pocket Books, 1960.

Rico, Gabriele Lusser. *Writing the Natural Way.* Los Angeles: J.P. Tarcher, Inc., 1983.

Tart, Charles T. *Waking Up: Overcoming the Obstacles to Human Potential.* Boston: New Science Library Shambhala, 1987.

· 3 ·

Goal Setting

When you are up to your armpits in alligators,
it's hard to remember that your original objective
was to drain the swamp.

—*Unknown*

The very act of reading this book indicates that you have a goal in mind. You may have already written your goal in the form of an affirmation. However, the purpose of this chapter to help you clarify your goal, become more specific and precise, and enhance your image of the goal. This will greatly increase the probability of success. Research indicates the one common characteristic of high level achievers is their ability to envision goals. It is really impossible to play with goals without using imagery, the topic of Part Two. Imagery and language overlap. Therefore, your goal statement will ultimately weave language with rich imagery.

Goal setting is a well-tested, proven methodology which can be learned rather easily. The purpose of the methodology is to produce goals which serve as valuable beacons to guide our way in creating the life we want. Periodic focus on goals reminds us of the original objective despite distractions. Life certainly holds a few surprise alligators! Goals are the blueprints, targets. Comparison of the "You are here" point to the goal provides the feedback needed to know if you are on the right path and if change of direction is needed to get back on course. Focus on a valued goal reminds one that the outcome is worth the price paid.

> Goals begin behaviors. Consequences maintain behaviors.
>
> —Blanchard & Johnson

Focus on a valued, specific *future* can immediately influence *present* action. This focus helps remain one that "Every action chooses the future" (Frances Vaughan).

The last point may be easily illustrated through experience. You may have discovered this in the eavesdropping exercise in the last chapter. Did you happen to come across a conversation on dieting or losing weight? What was the central theme of the conversation? Did it happen to be food or recipes? Talking about food and recipes means that attention is on food. Discussions of food elicit very rich imagery . . . taste, smell, sight . . . which in turn trigger all those wonderful associations we discovered in the mind-mapping exercise. Imagery also triggers strong physiologic response, most commonly salivation. However, it also can decrease blood-sugar level because the pancreas secretes insulin in response to the imagery. The body adjusts to the anticipated ingestion of food. "Aren't you hungry right now?" acts to trigger the same kind of response. Well, you *weren't* hungry, but you are now! The result is true physiological hunger. This is visceral learning.

The focus on food has undermined the goal (to be trim) in two ways: 1) hunger was stimulated and 2) associations for a particular food were activated. Hunger is a natural biological signal to begin eating, a necessity for meeting the needs of the body. One *should* eat when hungry. However, there is no need to stimulate hunger through thoughts of choice.

Associations are more difficult to deal with because one becomes hungry for a specific food. However, this problem can be alleviated by changing the thought/ discussion to include "appropriate" food (which almost never happens) or to focus on the goal . . . shift the conversation to types of workouts, progress toward the goal, etc. Willingly shifting attention to the goal orders consciousness. Remember, "Attention shapes the self, and is in turn shaped by it" (Csikszentmihalyi).

To voluntarily engage in conversations of this nature is self-indulgent and counterproductive. It is playing with fire. If you try to explain this to others, they will probably laugh it off because they do not understand the power of language and imagery. Thought represented through language and imagery can be channeled to produce powerful positive energy just as water is channeled to produce electricity. Conversely, it can run wildly and be destructive just like a flood.

Unfortunately, this power is subtle inasmuch as it does not have the concreteness of water. Plus, the power is usually governed by sloppy, habitually negative thought patterns. One must be consistently vigilant to govern consciously, to be awake. Focusing on the goal is being awake. Attention insures proper use of one's inherent powers of thought.

However, goals can be destructive when an individual is unaware of the effect of the goal in the context and totality of one's life or when the goal completely overshadows the the process of attainment. The goal is a place on the map; it is not the trip.

I ran into an acquaintance I had not seen for several months and was struck by her much leaner appearance and the vitality she exuded. I told her she looked terrific, to which she responded in an exasperated tone, "Yeah, but I'm not 110 yet." I responded, "So what? You look great!" She reiterated, "But I'm not 110!" Why is an increment on a scale important?

This woman did not know she had actually reached her goal of looking good because she could only "see" the goal in term of a scale. A television commercial for a national weight-control organization showed the elated expressions of their successul members as they saw the sliding metal indicator of the scale hit the magical increment. The last woman in the sequence hugs the scale! Perhaps the media contributes to this type of fixation. Appropriate goal vision is the ability to see and feel the goal within the context of your life. We will work on putting the goal in context in many different ways.

When an individual becomes obsessed with a goal or is too goal-oriented, the goal becomes more important than the process of living. The process is "now," which is actually the only real time we have. The past is done and the future only exists in our minds. A goal is merely a picture of the future. Goal obsession can crowd out enjoyment of the simplest life pleasures. As Leo Buscaglia stated, "Life is not a destination. Life is a trip." The purpose then is to have the goal stimulate appropriate action and guide process. Obsession is the antithesis of control because the thoughts control the individual rather than the individual controlling the thoughts.

Now, let's work on the process of clarifying goals, developing precision, and putting goals in context. You are working on creating your blueprint which will become your future. A treasure is created with this blueprint in which every one of us will benefit as it comes to life. Turn the page for Exercise One.

EXERCISE ONE

Context, Enrichment, & Expectation. Write your goal statement down in your journal.

Now, ask yourself . . .

"Can I see myself at this goal?"

"What will it feel like to be this goal?"

"How will my life be different?"

"What kinds of things will I do, having accomplished the goal, that I don't do now?"

"How will my relationships change?"

"How will my health be affected by this goal?"

"How will my family be affected by this goal?"

"How will my work be affected by this goal?"

"Will I be a 'better' person when I achieve this goal?"

"Will working toward this goal help me express my potential in other areas of my life?"

> One of the best ways to make something happen is to predict it.
> —Bernie Siegel

You can compare your expectations expressed in these answers with reality when you have achieved your goal.

Note that many of these questions force one to think in terms of the context of the goal . . . how will the acquistion of the goal influence the totality of life? They also act to expand and enrich your vision of the goal.

EXERCISE TWO

The Starting Point. There is general agreement that goal setting should start by determining the starting point. This allows you to choose the most appropriate solution and allows you to measure progress. Obviously, if there is no progress or if progress is too slow, the solution needs to be altered. Also, evidence of progress is motivating.

Scientific method calls for objective measurement. This is easier and more precise than subjective measurement.

1. Record your weight and your measurements. If possible, determine your body-fat percentage.

It is important to do a variety of measurements. Body weight is limited because it does not distinguish between fat loss/gain or water loss/gain. Many universities, health clubs, sports medicine clinics, and hospitals do body-fat percentages. Weigh yourself no more than once a week, the same day of the week at the same time of day— Monday at 7 a.m., for example.

The other "measurements" are subjective. That is, there is no direct measurement, but these subjective measures are more important in terms of the quality of one's life than any objective measure.

2. Describe your body. Do not read further until you have done so.

Interestingly, research showed that men objectively followed instructions for doing this exercise. They tend to describe their bodies. "I'm 5'10", medium build, brown, curly hair." Women, on the other hand, describe

Continued →

Exercise Two—cont'd.

what they don't like. "I have saddlebags and cellulite on my thighs." If you were meeting a stranger at the airport, chances are the male description would be adequate enough to identify the individual. It might be difficult to identify a woman strictly on the basis of saddlebags. Could someone identify you on the basis of your description?

3. Look at yourself in a full length mirror. Focus on your body as a whole and then focus on each part . . . eyes, ears, nose, hands, etc.

A. Then, write down what you *like* about your body and, if possible, describe why. This may be difficult, for we are not accustomed to seeing the beauty in ourselves.

B. Also, write down what you appreciate about your body. Do you appreciate the body's ability to heal itself, to get well, to grow and regenerate fingernails and toenails, to reproduce, to give pleasure?

There are a couple of reasons for doing this exercise. Self-love and liking are essential to foster the ability to nurture ourselves. We need to find things we like about ourselves. We need to learn to love and appreciate the miracle of our physical selves. This allows our perception to include the things most often overlooked.

C. Write down what you do not like about your body. Then ask yourself which of these things can realistically be changed.

EXERCISE THREE

The "Before" Picture

1. Take a picture of yourself. You may have to grit your teeth for this one, but this is not meant to be a punishment. It is another way to measure your starting point and to determine what you wish to change.

When John Travolta was preparing for his role as a dancer in the movie *Staying Alive,* they took a series of "before" pictures. They then compared his physique to the physiques of professional dancers to determine what he needed to do to make him look the part. They developed his entire fitness/ dietary regime for the purpose of fashioning a rather ordinary body into that of a sleek, lean, graceful dancer. John Travolta is noted for his dedication and commitment to a role. He had a phenomenally vigorous training program, the results of which where dramatically presented on screen. The movie was his "after" picture.

The fact is that we don't really see ourselves when we look in the mirror each day. We need the perspective of a camera to help reveal a different reality. We become a more objective observer with film.

2. Compare your picture to pictures of bodies which represent your ideal. Scan pictures in magazines and catalogs, picking out the ones you like. Or your ideal may be a picture of yourself as you were at a younger age. At first, there is no need to consider limitations. After you have gathered a collection, then match them to your general frame and possible composition. If you cannot find a realistic model, then make one up by creating a composite or try to sketch

Continued →

Exercise Three—cont'd.

a model. The idea is to expand your perception of what might be possible as well as to be realistic without imposing unnecessary limitations. A good trick, indeed. This exercise will help people who have difficulty imaging their ideal.

Investigate possibilities and begin to celebrate your own particular uniqueness. Appreciate the dyamics of the body and its incredible adaptability. There is no need to buy into the idea that the "cookie cutter" bodies the media foists upon the public is THE STANDARD of beauty. To accept the illusion that this standard is the only one worthy of sexual attraction, love, and wealth is to negate the wonderful gift of individuality.

Comparison of "model" bodies is meant to stimulate insights into your own possibilities, not to hook you into "The Standard." The only important standard is the one you create. As you begin to embrace your uniqueness, the special micro-universe of energy that is you, you will also begin to accept and celebrate others' uniqueness. Tune into the universal divinity of all the forms life takes, including your own. When you begin self-acceptance you will be able to quit trying so hard to be like everybody else. Jackie Gleason said, "Thin people are beautiful, but fat people are adorable." Expression of creative energies brings both.

By now, you should have a pretty clear idea picture of what you want.

EXERCISE FOUR

Write Your Goal Statement. Instead of the short affirmation, the goal statement will include other components to stimulate imagery and enthusiasm. For example, "I, Jonathan, will be 170 pounds by November 30. I know that I have the ability to achieve my goal, and my belief is so strong that I can see myself before the mirror looking my best—strong, healthy, happy, and lean. I promise myself that I will do everything possible to achieve my goal. When I reach my goal, I shall maintain it with all the vigor and commitment needed to do so."

_____
(signature)

You may decide to use this basic form. Change words to fit your concept of the goal. One client, for example, changed "lean" to "thin." She could see herself as thin but not lean.

Use the goal statement just as you would an affirmation until you reach your goal.

EXERCISE FIVE

Chunking the Goal. Break the goal down into manageable chunks by writing weekly and monthly goals. For weight loss, the goal should be no more than two pounds per week. "I will be 198 by Monday." Jonathan would not write, "I will lose two pounds by Monday." Write "I will be 190 by August 1" rather than "I will lose eight pounds by August 1." The first forms elicit the images of success. The second forms focus too much on the process of "losing" weight. Process is more effectively manipulated through imagery of burning fat, increasing metabolism, etc., which will be addressed thoroughly later.

Always use both the original long-term goal with the short-term goals. A group of cameramen and reporters were assembled at the summit of a mountain to record the victory of the first woman ever to accomplish the climb. Someone asked, "What did you think about while you scaled this mountain?" She replied, "I kept repeating to myself, 'You eat an elephant one bite at a time.'" Her response reflected the meaning of an Alcoholics Anonymous axiom which is to take one day at a time. This wisdom carries over to the goals of weight control. Oftentimes when we look at the long road ahead, the immensity of the task we are considering is overwhelming. We feel exhausted and defeated even before we begin the journey.

Counselor: "Can you lose 100 pounds?"

Client: "Well, I don't know."

Counselor: "Can you lose a pound in four days?"

Client: "Of course."

Continued →

Exercise Five—cont'd.

Counselor: "Then a pound at a time you will lose 100 pounds in about one year."

The short-term goal reduces the task to a perspective that seems easier and possible.

The martial arts deal with goals very effectively with a ranking system indicated by belt color. The novice participates as a no-belt or white belt. At the beginning of the class, students line up according to rank, white belts at the back of the room, then yellow, green, etc. Black, the highest rank, is at the front. The novice knows that if he/she works diligently he/she could possibly be a black belt in three or four years. It is a long road with much sweat and a few injuries. Three years seems like an eternity to a child! It would be extremely easy to get discouraged early in the game. However, the novice knows that, in two or three months, there is a promotion test. Proudly, one moves up to yellow belt. The novice sees the black belts every day, which is a constant reminder of the long-term goal. But today is for work toward the yellow belt. Finally, one reaches the black. It is an ingenious system for motivating students on a continual basis without ever even mentioning the word "goal."

There is a lesson to be learned from this system. We need to break our long-term goals down into short- and intermediate-range goals while also being reminded of the ultimate goal. Further, we need to recognize and celebrate each level of accomplishment.

EXERCISE SIX

Celebrating Accomplishments. Brainstorm a list of rewards you will give yourself for achieving short-term goals. They should be simple and inexpensive, such as going to a movie, buying an album, taking a hike in the woods, etc. Plan something extra special for achieving the ultimate: a trip to Mexico, a new wardrobe, etc. Learn to celebrate accomplishments without food or with appropriate food choices so that you begin building new associations. The reward system is only meaningful if given following the accomplishment. If you get the treat anyway, what is the point?

EXERCISE SEVEN

Action Goals. What will you DO today, this week, to achieve your goal? If you engage in appropriate action, the goal will take care of itself. As Tom Hopkins, a sales trainer of national repute, said, "You already have the goal; it just hasn't arrived yet." This sounds unbelievably simplistic, but you need to remember this when you hit a snag. Weight loss can be unpredicable because of variations in water retention, muscle mass, salt intake, etc. Even if you have a thorough knowledge of the variables influencing weight, it is discouraging to discover that there is no physical evidence of success when you have worked very hard. The influence of these different variables even out in the long run and you will eventually see the physical evidence if you continue acting appropriately. You can avoid the discouragement of the inevitable plateaus by focusing on your action. Action has consequence. You just may not be able to see it yet.

> Only action gives to life its strength, its joy,
> its purpose. . . . Act or ye will be acted upon.
> —Og Mandino

What is "appropriate" action? What program should one follow? It is beyond the scope of this book to deal with diet and exercise plans. There are many good plans and many horrible plans. Any good food plan should include variety and balance. I tend to favor programs like the Pritikin Program or Dean

Continued →

Exercise Seven—cont'd.

Ornish's *Program for Reversing Heart Disease* because they are low in fat and high in complex carbohydrates. Therefore, it is not necessary to count calories (a totally unnatural act!), plus the variety of friuts, vegetables, and grains insure adequate vitamin and fiber intake. One gets to eat without restricting quantity as long as choice is correct. Also, all programs of weight loss should include an exercise plan. If the plan claims there is no need for exercise, then the red flag is up . . . there is no need for that program. See the recommended reading at the end of the chapter for suggestions.

EXERCISE EIGHT

A booster shot for goals. On one side of a note card write down all the consequences of being at your ideal weight. On the other side, write down all the consequences of not obtaining you weight goal. Read the card before you eat anything.

This helps you focus on the many aspects of consequence of an action precisely at the time it is needed. Some people are motivated by the positive consequences goals bring while others are motivated to move away from the negative consequences. Which way are you motivated? If you don't know, use both sides of the card. If you know, use the side that fits your preference.

No doubt you have discovered that goal setting takes thoughtful consideration. It is one of the first and most important steps in taking control of one's life. Keep in mind, however, that goals are not written in stone. It is perfectly acceptable to change and even abandon goals when they no longer contribute to one's growth. And, although the goals written here always contain a deadline, the progress toward the goal is always more important than meeting the deadline.

I applaud all who commit to challenging goals. The very fact that they are challenging means that there is an inherent risk of failure. I think it is perfectly acceptable to set goals which push the limits of other people's belief systems as long as you believe in yourself. However, to set and strive for exceedingly

Continued →

Exercise Eight—cont'd.

difficult, challenging goals requires two conditions. One, you are patient. This means that failure to meet a deadline does not destroy your resolve. And two, you can forgive yourself when you make mistakes. In the words of Ghandi, "Be forgiving of your own evolution." Failure is only one kind of feedback and, if you don't give up, you have not really failed.

Suggested Reading:

Fritz, Robert. *The Path of Least Resistance.* Salem, MA: BMA, Inc., Stillpoint Publishing, 1984.

Ornish, Dean. *Program for Reversing Heart Disease.* New York: Ballantine Books, 1990.

·4·

The Working Ideal: Building Motivational Muscle

How different our lives are when we really know what is deeply important to us, and, keeping that picture in mind, we manage ourselves each day to be and to do what really matters most. If the ladder is not leaning against the right wall, every step we take just gets us to the wrong place faster.

—Stephen R. Covey

All of our behavior, simple to complex, is our best attempt to . . . satisfy our needs. . . .

—William Glasser

There was a time in my life when I was the most miserable, unhappy, depressed, and desperate person I had ever met. It was after reading my journal which I had kept for several years that I concluded that I would never achieve what I wanted with my life if I continued life with the same recurrent patterns of depression and lethargy. This realization hit me like a thunderbolt. I was afraid. It was then I decided to do something. Of course, at the time I did not have a clue as to what to do and wasn't at all sure I had the energy to do what I needed to do even if I figured it out.

I started reading everything I could get my hands on that related to personal transformation. That was the beginning of a personal adventure of excitement, enthusiasm, fear, impatience, and frustration. At one point when I was working with a little book of affirmations, I became so frustrated and angry that I threw the blickity-blank book across the room in a rage. "This garbage may work but it sure as hell isn't working for me!"

A few hours later I picked up the book and began again. Affirmations did not seem to be working, but the concept made sense to me and I believed it should work.

Through my journal I learned that I had a history of negative thought patterns which were slowly sapping my energy and my ability to cope. I was surviving, but I was no place close to thriving. My one saving grace was that I really wanted to thrive. I wanted it even more when I learned through my research that people could actually *learn* how to thrive. What you are reading and the techniques you are working with in this book are things I either created or discovered during the work I was, and am still, doing for myself. I have merely related the knowledge and skills to weight and body- composition control.

A few years ago, I developed my goals, taped them to the wall, read them over and over again, imagined them . . . all the things I asked you to do in the previous chapter on goal setting. At first, I was enthused and eager, but I found with time some of the enthusiasm and eagerness diminished. What was the problem here? The goals certainly did not vary in their importance.

When one is hopeful and energized, commitment is high. Commitment is directly proportional to energy and hope. Therefore, it is not surprising that commitment varies from day to day, even hour to hour. Rating yourself on a scale of 0 to 10, what is your level of commitment for achieving your goal *right now?* What is it at 7 a.m., at 3 p.m., at 10 p.m., when you are out to dinner with friends, when you are celebrating your birthday, when you are tired, when you are sick?

As long as you are in a resourceful state—that is, feeling good and strong—commitment is usually higher than when you are in an unresourceful state. Success requires consistency and persistence. Natural lows undermine those essential attributes of success.

How do we get through these unresourceful periods successfully, maintaining positive behavior to insure the outcome we truly want in the long run? William Glasser stated, ". . . we always choose to do what is most satisfying to us at the time." Many of society's problems stem from people satisfying themselves "at the time." Ideally, we want to choose to do what is most satisfying to us in the context of the totality of our lives, not "at the time." Ideally, the working ideal can help us see the meaning and consequences of choice within the context of this totality.

The purpose of developing and using the working ideal is to tap into our motivations and strengthen our resolve for the long haul. I discovered that the working ideal was a perpetual source of personal power when I could relate my goals to the foundation of the ideal. It kept commitment high. A resolution was truly a resolution because the ideal gave the goal meaning in the context of my life, my life with others, my life with the earth and all earth's critters.

So, what is a working ideal? Edgar Cayce explained the ideal:

> The standard of quality of motivation by which we measure our decisions and actions . . . Setting an ideal is establishing a quality of spirit that is related to motivation, desire, purpose, intention, and incentive. It provides a measuring rod by which to make comparisons, but it is also an internal centering which automatically gives us a clearer perception of every issue . . . Probably the most important aspect of our lives is proper motivation and establishing a criterion of our purpose; i.e., an ideal. (1982)

One of the easiest ways to identify an ideal is to answer the question, "What standards guide my behavior?" "What defines 'right' behavior versus 'wrong' behavior?"

Society and government have standards which identify "right" versus "wrong" behavior. The United States Constitution is the standard for government, the law. Laws are questioned with, "Is it constitutional?" "Is it my constitutional right?" I get to say anything I want because the constitution guarantees me the right to freedom of speech. The Constitution reflects our value of individual liberty.

Religions have standards which identify "right" behavior. The Ten Commandments identify wrong behavior in the "Thou shalt nots . . ." The Golden Rule is a standard of behavior. The Bible, the Koran, the Talmud, the Book of Mormon, and so on all establish standards of right behavior.

Your standard will be a composite of what you have been taught, what you have accepted, and what your personal experience and feeling dictate as important and valued. To clarify, a personal example follows:

One part of my personal ideal is to do nothing to create suffering in any living being, to alleviate unnecessary suffering wherever possible, and to do nothing to support others who perpetuate suffering. I've had this ideal, in its rough form, since I was 13 when I saw many of my animals die of parasitic infestation. As I matured I became aware of all the little things I did which created suffering. So I had an ideal based on the compassion I felt for my pets, and I had it before I ever wrote it down. My ideal is now more refined and my actions more all-encompassing. I do not eat animals. This action did not start until I was about 28.

It took 15 years to expand the action and consciousness of compassion and make the connection between suffering and my eating habits. Once I made the connection, I never once missed eating meat. The opportunity to eat meat is never a temptation precisely because of the ideal and its personal value to me. There is no feeling of deprivation.

Let's use another example which applies directly to weight control. Suppose that part of Jo's ideal is "To respect and love myself and others."

Assuming that Jo understands the negative effects of high dietary fat intake, her choice to limit fat intake is a manifestation of her self-respect and love. Her realization that her choice is part of a larger principle upon which she lives her life reduces the pain she might otherwise feel in "giving up" rich foods.

An ideal, or part of an ideal, may develop as a natural outcome of experience. Or it may take some conscious soul reaching and creativity to develop and to recognize connections between ideals and actions. Once defined, the gratification of maintaining personal integrity is much more rewarding than momentary appeasement.

The ideal makes action easier precisely because it is the ideal that is important. If an ideal includes, "To treat others as I wish to be treated," then it is easy to be kind and giving. There is no sacrifice because whatever is "given up" is given up for a higher value. Trading a beaten-up 1969 heap for this year's model is not a sacrifice because this year's model is more valuable.

Let's give it a go and begin the process.

EXERCISE ONE

Standards of "Right" Behavior.
A. Write down any standard that guides you in determining right behavior. You may wish to outline this or write it in a paragraph.

If you have a difficult time with this, examine your religious beliefs. The following are examples from some of my students and clients.

To do my best; to strive for excellence

To keep an open mind; to be respectful of all people without regard to their color, sex, age, etc.

To respect myself

To treat others as I wish to be treated

To be happy

To be loving

To act on what I know

To contribute more to the world than I take away

To be honest

To always be supportive of my family and friends

B. Define any abstract terms. Precision is important and necessary for application. For purpose of example, to be loving means to nurture my own and other people's growth toward our best potentials.

Definition helps in the pinch of dilemma. Suppose a good friend comes to you for a loan. *Another* loan! Giving is certainly a demonstration of love, but perhaps the friend is taking advantage of you. In this case, the loan would not contribute to your growth or his. He becomes weaker with each loan and cannot stand on his own. You become poorer. By definition then, to loan him the money is wrong

Continued →

Exercise One—cont'd.

action. The only way to determine if the action is right or wrong is through definition. Notice how the ideal is functioning to ". . . give us a clearer perception of the every issue." Without knowing the ideal and its meaning, how would you know what to do?

C. Does your ideal cover all situations life offers? If it doesn't, you are not done. To be honest is an admirable ideal, but it only covers certain situations. It would not cover the loan example given above. Expand the ideal to include more. You will find that the parts of the ideal will interact with each other.

EXERCISE TWO

Fitting goals to the foundation. Suppose my ideal is a) to be loving; i.e., to contribute to my own and other people's growth towards their best potentials; b) to strive for excellence; i.e., I will do my best work; and c) to act on what I know.

What does this have to do with losing weight or maintaining an ideal weight? Maybe nothing. However, when the goal is a manifestation of the ideal in some way, the goal automatically becomes more important and more highly prized. The goal springs from motive (internal, inside yourself) instead of from incentive (external, outside yourself). This means you are in control of it, for it is from you . . . you are creating it.

See if you can feel the difference in the power of these two examples.

1) "I am going to lose 10 pounds by Christmas because we are going to the Bahamas and I want to look good in my new swimsuit."

2) "I am going to lose 10 pounds by Christmas because I think I'll feel better about myself and I'll have more energy."

Example #1 is an incentive. Incentives do encourage movement toward a goal and can be used effectively. However, when the incentive is lost, so is the action. I once had a client who had this incentive. She and her husband were going to go on a cruise and she wanted to lose 20 pounds. She was progressing nicely until the plans for the cruise fell through. Her disappointment led her right back to her

Continued →

Exercise Two—cont'd.

original weight and then some.

Example #2 is a motivation, the need for self-respect and the freedom respect brings with it. It can easily be connected to the ideal of "To be loving" for the goal is a natural expression and manifestation of self-love. One can more easily realize potential with energy than without energy.

"Is your goal an expression of your ideal?" If it is, you are more likely to achieve it especially when you activate the ideal by thinking about it. Are your other goals expressions of your ideal?

EXERCISE THREE

"Work" the Ideal. I discovered the ideal from Edgar Cayce. I added the "working" to the "Working Ideal" because the ideal is only useful when one activates it. One must make it work just as one makes affirmations work. First, you must write it down. Writing forces you to be precise and clear in your thinking. As W. H. Auden stated, "How can I know what I think till I see what I say?"

Again, this entails self-discovery.

I am always somewhat amazed by the ideals my students write. This is one of their more difficult assignments because the majority of them have never given this much thought. It also requires sophisticated cognitive skills. They do have ideals, and admirable ones. The effort is in pinning it down and ironing out vagueness with precision. I also tell them that if they do not have an ideal to make one up and try it on. See if it works for you. I find I usually like them more after reading this assignment. Most of the time, much like the rest of us, they fly by the seats of their pants and act in much the same way. That is exactly why they get into trouble. If only we would think of the consequence of action in the context and totality of our lives, what a difference we would see in the designs of those lives! WRITE IT DOWN.

Second, dwell on the ideal just as you do affirmations, the goal statement, and the goal image. It will improve your consistency. You will be tougher and commitment will fluctuate less. Read your ideal over and over and over again until you automatically act

Continued →

Exercise Three—cont'd.

on it. Repeat it until it is as much a part of your sub-consciousness as it is your waking consciousness. You will only get stronger.

Suggested Reading:

Covey, Stephen R. *The 7 Habits of Highly Effective People.* New York: Simon & Schuster, 1989.

PART II

IMAGERY

It is imagination that gives shape to the universe.
—Barry Lopez

Your imaginings can have as much power over you
as your reality, or even more.
—Charles Tart

·5·

Imagery:
The Power Source

"Before words, images were . . ."
"Visualization is not just an idea; it is one half
of consciousness. It is one way we think, perhaps
the more basic way."
—*Samuels & Samuels*

Imagery is the most creative force innately available to human beings. Consciously and unconsciously, thought takes the form of images, an expression of our natural birthright. Just as with language, images may act to either order or disorder consciousness. An image of a cure for cancer or AIDS may be the seed for its realization and the channeling of a researcher's energies toward its fulfillment. Or relentless, recurrent images of disaster may render one powerless and helpless, immobilized in fear and drained of energy. We can imagine ourselves as

79

worthy, successful champions or as losers. The image becomes the self-fulfilling prophecy.

Again, as with language, images come as if by their own volition. It is when we learn to fashion, transform, and redirect images that we begin to get a glimpse of the power held in this form of thought. Whether the power of imagination is used for benefit or destruction is a matter of choice. Whether it is a friend or foe depends upon proper use. The sad fact is that most of us just do not know how to use this gift. Misuse leads to failure, misery, anger, and frustration. Proper use leads to the fulfillment of our best possible potentials.

The purpose of this section to learn to unleash the power of imagination by transforming images into positive energy. Specifically, you will learn to use imagery to:

1) increase the probability of success

2) increase will power

3) change your perception, which will function to change the meaning of events and objects

4) literally change your physiology in order to increase metabolism, burn fat easier, control hunger and appetite, and establish a lower biological weight naturally.

What is this innate ability? Let's establish exactly what imagery is by way of experience.

Think about the kitchen in your house. Can you describe the floor covering, the furniture arrangement, the color of the cabinets and curtains, the arrangement of utensils and canisters, the location of the can opener, the smell of coffee brewing, the dish cloth? Which way do the door and windows open; what kind of latches are on the cabinets; what is in the refrigerator; what does the floor feel like against your bare feet? Is it carpeted? Is it linoleum? What is the texture? Is the floor warm, cool, or cold? Is the floor clean, or do crumbs stick to the bottoms of your feet? Describe the atmosphere. When you think about your kitchen, is there anyone present in the room with you? Who is it? How do you feel in the kitchen when you're alone or hungry or with friends or family? Listen. What do you hear? The fan, the hum of the refrigerator, traffic noise, birds?

You are able to reconstruct your kitchen from your memory almost as if you were actually standing in the center of the room. You can use all your senses—vision, hearing, smell, touch, and even taste. You can even experience the "feeling" of the room by remembering variations of the conditions of the environment. You experience emotion. This is imagery or, as it is sometimes called, visualization. So you see, you naturally have this ability.

People do, however, have variations in their ability to experience the full range of imagery. For example, some people *see* vivid, colorful images almost as through they were standing right there in their kitchen with their eyes opened. A few people don't *see* images at all but have a keen sense of the object, place, or event. One client described an object as bright red. However, he explained that he did not actually *see* red, whereupon I asked, "Well then, how did you know it was red?" He replied, "I *sensed* its redness." As a person with vivid visual imagery, I am not sure what he meant. Language often fails to describe experience and feeling. The important point here is that he could and did successfully use imagery despite the fact that it was not precisely visual.

So, if you could not experience all of the sensations suggested in the kitchen example, you probably experienced it in some form well enough to accurately describe and experience your kitchen. This means you are successful with imagery. There is no human in the world with a functioning brain who does not use imagery and imagination.

To take the exercise two steps further, put yourself back in your kitchen. Imagine standing in the middle of the room. Walk over to the refrigerator and take out a crisp, cool apple. If you happen to be fresh out of apples, take the liberty of creative license. Hold the apple in your hand, bring it up close to your face, and look at it carefully. Notice the color. Turn it around in the light and look at it from all angles. Does it shine or is it dull? Notice the texture. Feel the peel, the shape, the temperature. Does it have a stem? Is it red, yellow, or green? Take the apple over to the counter and slice it with a knife. Bring the apple close to your nose and inhale slowly and deeply. Taste it. Chew it up and swallow. Feel it go right down into your stomach.

Two things happened in this exercise. One, environment was manipulated through imagination by way of suggestion. There are several terms for this type of suggestion, including guided imagery, guided visualization, fantasy, or guided fantasy. Something was literally created in your mind that was not there before. Two, even though the image was not "real," a body response occurred as though it were real. Had you been hooked up to the appropriate equipment, we would find that 1) your eyes moved as you looked at the apple, 2) your muscles moved slightly in exactly the same pattern they would actually move as you walked to the refrigerator and counter, 3) you salivated and your masticator muscles tensed, and 4) you may have increased gastric secretion in the stomach.

This simple exercise clearly demonstrates the connection between the body and the mind. Remember the body-mind connection was summarized by a statement made by the pioneers of biofeedback, Elmer and Alyce Green of the Menninger Clinic:

> . . . every change in the mental emotional state, conscious or unconscious, is accompanied by an appropriate change in the physiological state.
> —Simonton, et al.,1978, p. 29

The body and mind function in relation with each other. When we affect one, we necessarily and unavoidably affect the other.

This connection can be extremely precise. Brown reported that individuals can "learn how to activate and suppress the activity of individual motoneurons in the spinal cord that control the activity of muscle cells" (Brown, 1980, p. 254). Brown and Simonton have both stated that people have learned to control every physiological function which can accurately be measured and fed back to them. In my studies with imagery and metabolism, *every* individual tested increased basal metabolic rate in 11 minutes without the measurement being fed back to them merely by thinking with appropriate images. You will learn how to do this through these exercises.

You may visualize the best or the worst. Successful people have learned to use imagery to their advantage by consciously and habitually imagining the best possible scenario. Whatever the image, it is a prediction of outcome.

When I was 10, my brother and I frequently visited a friend on his farm. These visits were wonderful times filled with the excitement and fun of being in the country, playing tag, hide-and-seek, and swimming.

There was a stream running through a pasture which, in the course of our play, we crossed many, many times. I distinctly remember standing on the river bank, looking for the most strategic arrangement of stones to serve as stepping stones for crossing the river without getting wet. In my mind's eye, I invariably saw myself slipping off one of the stones and getting my shoes and socks wet. And sure enough, every time, I did!

Of course, at 10, it never occurred to me that I could or should change my image. Each failure reinforced the negative expectation for the next time. Creating negative images was as much a part of my habitual thought pattern as was negative language.

When I told a friend about this childhood experience at the farm, he said, "Well then, you know something about imagery, don't you?" I did not know what he was getting at. I asked, "What do I know?" He answered, "Imagery works."

The task is to get it to work the way we want and need it to work. The next chapter deals specifically with the use of imagery at different levels. To get to the actual work of imagery, use the next chapter, "Levels of Imagery," along with the chapter "The Personal Power Pack." The last chapter in Part II, "Assets and Liabilities," deals with the handling of specific problems and concerns plus ways to improve the effectiveness of one's imagery.

Suggested Reading:

Brown, Barbara. *Super-Mind*. New York: Bantam Books, 1980.

Gawain, Shakti. *Creative Visualization*. New York: Bantam Books, 1978.

Samuels, Mike and Samuels, Nancy. *Seeing with the Mind's Eye*. New York: Random House, 1975.

·6·

Levels of Imagery

When the will and the imagination are in conflict, imagination always wins.
                                    —*Emile Coué*

There are varying degrees of imagery from the gross to the very subtle. In this sense, "gross" means large, big, or bulky. "Subtle" means fine and delicate. Division of imagery into levels is an arbitrary means of practically dealing with a wide range of experience. It helps systematically order objectives and practice. For our purposes, I identify the levels of imagery as gross, cellular, and nutritional.

Gross Imagery

Gross imagery is imagery in context. The most common example of gross imagery is the example we used in the chapter on goal setting where language and imagery where used together. However, the first exercise here will guide you through more specifics which will make your imagery more powerful.

EXERCISE ONE

The Goal Image. There are two ways to do these exercises. The first is to read the exercise, close your eyes, then let it happen. The second and probably the more effective is to record the exercises on a tape and play them back. You may wish to make your own tape. Details on this will be given later.

Select a quiet, comfortable spot where you will not be interrupted. The first time through, I suggest you sit up so that your spine is straight, in a chair, cross-legged, whatever is comfortable. Once you know the script, you may lie down unless you have a tendency to fall asleep.

I have occasionally had clients who experience a great deal of restlessness or irritability when asked to "assume a quiet attitude, to be still." If you experience this after a few practice sessions, do the activity standing, gently rocking back and forth from one foot to the other, or walk around slowly in any direction or pattern. Restrict the area of movement, because, at this point, it is important to keep your eyes closed. This decreases external stimulation and helps turn your attention inward toward thought and feeling.

Take your time. Give yourself as much time as you need to see and feel the images presented. If

Continued →

Exercise One—cont'd.

you deviate from the exercise, that is perfectly all right. If your mind wanders, don't worry about it. Just gently "push" the unwanted images to the side, out of sight, and continue.

Now, in your mind's eye, follow the script:

Focus on the breath . . . the air moving gently in and out . . . with each out breath, let all the tension go. I am peaceful and calm.

Alone in a dark, comfortable and safe theater sitting next to a movie projector, I am in complete control of the images on the screen. On the screen I now see myself as I am at my goal . . . strong, healthy, happy, and confident. I see myself at home . . . at work . . . with my family. I see myself doing things with exceptional confidence and vitality. I am wearing the clothes I have always wanted to wear. Movement is incredibly easy. I move effortlessly.

Now, instead of just watching myself doing these things on the screen, I AM doing them in real life . . . I walk into the screen and actually participate. I not only see, but I feel, touch, taste, and smell. I see myself with a strong, healthy, and lean body. I feel my energy and vitality in this wonderfully adaptable body. I appreciate the wonders and feats of this marvelous body which allows me to enjoy my relationship with myself, family, friends, animals, and the world. I am happy. I experience myself at work with my colleagues . . . with my family . . . with my friends.

They are happy for me and give me compliments, which I gladly accept. I deserve their recognition.

Continued →

Exercise One—cont'd.

I look at myself in the mirror and observe my body . . . I observe each part of my body with its appropriate leanness and muscle tone. Touching my body, I feel its tone. The muscles are firm and the skin tone is beautiful. I am happy. I feel good and energetic.

Focus on the breath for a few moments. Open the eyes slowly.

Explanation of Exercise One

Besides gross imagery, you began the exercise with a brief relaxation induction. Since we all do imagery all the time, an introductory relaxation technique may seem superfluous. However, relaxation is extremely important with this kind of work. Relaxation techniques quiet the left hemisphere of the mind, the language side of the brain.

Gabriele Rico (1983) called the left brain "the judge." It is the critic that will dredge up the old language scripts which may negate and interfere with both the ability to create new images and denigrate the existing ones. Analysis and judgment are the death knells of creative imagery. Rico stated that you should put "the judge" on the chair next to you and tell it to be quiet. It will get its say, but later. A relaxation induction is one way to effectively put the judge on the chair and keep it quiet. Also, quieting the left brain allows one to "hear" the right brain. The right hemisphere of the brain is the intuitive, imagery, insightful side. The right brain allows us to see a problem or event in the context of the whole. It allows us to see patterns. In the beginning, guided imagery is best performed in a quiet, comfortable place to facilitate greater involvement of the right hemisphere of the brain.

Once you have solidly imprinted a repertoire of successful images, you will be able to do them anywhere in milliseconds. Totie Fields once stated that, all the while she was doing her Las Vegas act on stage, she was thinking about what she was going to have for dinner after the show, right down to the pizza toppings. When you can quickly and frequently focus on the details of your goal with similar facility while in a variety of environments, you can eliminate the relaxation phase altogether.

You practiced two types of imagery: dissociated (objective) and associated (subjective). Dissociated imagery is viewing the image from a distance as an observer, as a member of an audience views a play. This is one perspective. You experience the play vicariously. Associated imagery is acting in the play . . . you are directly experiencing the action. This is yet another perspective. Both are valuable in learning to manipulate and play with imagery. Associated imagery is probably the most effective in changing physiology.

In this exercise, the only physiology that will change is that you will experience a more resourceful state because you will be more hopeful and confident. This is an extremely important change, for this resourceful state is what actually gives you the energy to carry out action goals . . . to do what you need to do to be successful.

EXERCISE TWO

Mental Rehearsal: "The Restaurant." Assume a comfortable position in your quiet, safe place. Close your eyes and focus on your breath. Release all tension with the out breath. Let go of everything you do not need . . . pain, anger, frustration . . . all gone with the breath. Count backwards from 25 to 0.

You are at a restaurant. As you look at the menu, you focus on all the truly good choices you can make. You only focus on good choices, ignoring the poor choices. When the waiter asks for your order, you happily ask for food that meets your needs. You have just given yourself a gift. You confidently ask how your order is prepared. The restaurant is there to serve you. You ask for your bread without butter, the meat to be broiled rather than fried, etc. You ask for what you need. You focus on and enjoy your companions and the atmosphere. There is much more to savor than just the food.

When you see your friends or family members make poor choices, you know that you need not feel deprived. They have not made the same choices you have and that is their decision. Your choices are your decision. You don't expect them to change because you have changed. They may have chosen to deprive their bodies through ignorance, rationalization, fear, or self-indulgence, or it may just be that their awareness is different. Their behavior does not determine your behavior. You are free to enjoy and savor your choices. Each choice determines your

Continued →

Exercise Two—Cont'd.

present and your future. Let the image go and focus on your breathing. Slowly and gently, in your own time, open your eyes.

Explanation of Exercise Two

The purpose of mental rehearsal is to imprint images of success which will increase self-confidence. It also activates the nervous system and helps establish proper neurological pathways necessary for the successful execution of skills. Mental rehearsal is a method of imagery used by successful athletes, astronauts, and business people. Basically, all it consists of is visualizing an event or situation going the way you want it to. A gymnast might visualize a perfect floor exercise routine; an astronaut, a perfectly executed drill; a business person, a presentation to a management team.

With eating behavior, many "dieters" dread social occasions because they know there will be food items available that they want but should not have. They are afraid they will be unable to resist the temptation. Dieters can use mental rehearsal to increase their ability to successfully deal with challenging situations just as athletes and business people do.

There are two ways to deal with the problems inherent in social situations. The most effective long-term solution is to change your perception so that you truly do not want the items you "shouldn't" have. You accomplish this through nutritional and cellular imagery, which we will discuss and practice later.

The other way is through mental rehearsal. Just as the gymnast visualizes the perfect floor-exercise routine, you visualize "perfect" performance at the restaurant. You use the same principles of imagery during mental rehearsal as you use in other visualization exercises.

Vividly imagine yourself in the situation looking over the menu, making the most positive choices, enjoying the company of your friends or family you are sharing your time with, and feeling good about your choices, knowing that these choices are bringing you closer to your goal with more self-esteem and confidence. When you combine the focus on the goal with the "reinforcement menu" and language with imagery, you have double-barreled firepower.

The nicest thing about mental rehearsal, whether it is used for developing a skill or changing behavior, is that you never need to make a mistake! You can practice it perfectly every time. Merely by practicing mentally, you can improve performance.

A study was done on the effects of mental rehearsal on making basketball free-throw performance that has become a classic. In a controlled study, one group practiced free-throw shots on a court for a specified period of time each day. Another group practiced for the same amount of time for the same number of days, but this group only practiced in their minds. They found that the first group which practiced actually shooting free throws on the court improved by 24 per cent. The mental-rehearsal group improved 23 per cent!

Perhaps even more exceptional are the prisoners of war who maintained their sanity by learning to play musical instruments without the instruments! They taught their bodies with their minds.

Granted, eating behavior is somewhat different because of the multitude of intervening variables, both physiological (hunger, blood-sugar levels, smell, taste) and psychological (associations with food, people). However, it is similar in that you eliminate mistakes and reinforce appropriate action by focusing on the goal.

You are also implementing suggestion. During the exercise, you are suggesting to yourself that you, in fact, *are* successful. Before you even arrive at the restaurant, you have suggested that you are happy and confident about positive choices. There is no indecision about what you are going to order and enjoy because the decision was already made minutes, hours, days, or even weeks before the event.

One of the most difficult aspects of dealing with obese individuals, especially individuals who have been overfat as children, is that they have never experienced success with their bodies. Their history is one of painful nicknames, nagging, rejection, and discrimination. Therefore, when they are successful, they do not *believe* the success. They may have a difficult time handling success and many times sabotage themselves in an unknowing effort to prove that they are failures rather than successes.

It is not surprising that one's actions parallel one's belief and value system. Through imagery, we can give ourselves a successful history so that we learn how success feels and can learn how to handle it in the present and future.

EXERCISE THREE

Mental Rehearsal: "Building a Successful History." You can practice any number of exercises to do this. Select an example from your personal history that was particularly painful or unpleasant. A common example is during physical education class when two or more captains of the teacher's choice choose their teams one by one until all students are selected. The heavy kids stand there praying to themselves that they won't be the last ones chosen . . . maybe second or third from the end, but not the last one! The affair is particularly humiliating because it is so blatantly public.

With mental rehearsal, you actively change your history by reliving the scene the way you want it to go. You are the producer, director, writer, and casting director. Write your own script. Take care to be totally positive in redoing your history. Be totally successful, a hero or champion, the captain or most valuable player.

Avoid the temptation to humiliate or be negative to any of the other characters. Revenge may be sweet, but it does not promote life and liveliness and, therefore, negates the positivity which we are trying to develop and nurture in ourselves. Be content with the wisdom of Mort Sahl who said, "Survival is the best revenge." "Thrival" is even better. Practice many situations with a sense of playfulness. The more success you experience via mental rehearsal, the more comfortable you will be with your victories, even the little ones.

EXERCISE FOUR

Mental Rehearsal: "Creating the Successful Scenario." In your journal, describe as many situations as you can think of where you were not successful. Give as much detail as possible. Some situations may be recurrent. You may binge after work, at 2 a.m., or snack after dinner. Merely describe a sample to represent this kind of situation. Other situations might be the traditional happy hour on Fridays, when you eat with friends, or when you are alone. Or perhaps the situation is a celebration such as a birthday, Thanksgiving, or Christmas. Then write out a scenario which counters the negative image. Think about what a person does and experiences who does not act out the negative image. For example, many people do not snack right after work. They may take the dog for a walk, work out, play tennis, read the paper, etc. They do these activities naturally without a sense deprivation, fear, or fear of loss of control. What would your "model" person do (dissociated imagery)? How would your "model" person feel? Then, step into the action with associated imagery and "see" yourself acting and feeling the same way.

Practice. Practice. Practice! You are building a successful history and establishing different neurological pathways of action each and every time you experience the imagery. It will take some time to make these patterns stronger than the old ones. Since each person is different, it is not possible to offer a script for you for this exercise. You are the sole creator here.

Continued →

Exercise Four—cont'd.

Some clients have expressed their fear of placing themselves in situations which challenge them, for they quite rightly expect the worst. They know from past experience that they lose control in these situations. They respond by avoiding the situations which trigger uncontrollable behavior. Of course, this is a pretty good idea in the beginning. However, avoidance is not practical or enjoyable as a lifestyle. Likewise, living in fear is painful. With mental rehearsal, the fear can be replaced with self-control and enjoyment.

Cellular Imagery

After working with weight control for two or three years, I discovered that the traditional solutions just did not work for many people. The "scientific" solution is profoundly simple: if one takes in fewer calories each day than one expends, weight loss occurs. This creates a caloric deficit which requires that the body supply fuel for energy from fat reserves. Since a pound of fat is worth 3500 calories, a deficit of 500 calories per day should result in a loss of one pound per week.

However, many dieters and counselors know that this fails to accurately predict weight loss in some people. Even the most committed, goal-directed individual is placed at a distinct disadvantage when he/she cannot lose weight or loses very slowly (1/4 to 1/2 pound per week) on as little as 700 calories per day with exercise. It is, therefore, not surprising when people give up. Why is it so difficult to create and maintain a deficit long enough to reach ideal weight? Why is it so difficult to maintain ideal weight once it is achieved?

Out of frustration, I began experimenting with other approaches. I am sincerely grateful to all those clients who willingly participated as pioneers in this new area of cellular imagery and to those people who participated in the first pilot studies on the effects of imagery on metabolism. But it was one person in particular who really stimulated ideas through her experiences. This was about four or five years before I actually had the opportunity to test these ideas on a scientific basis.

J.P. was about 100 pounds overweight. Since her progress was so poor, I asked her to try to imagine changing her set point. The technique was not very sophisticated, for I did not know much about imagery at the time. So she pretty much came up with the image herself. She imaged that her biologically assigned weight (set point) was set too high. Just as if a thermostat was set too high, she turned the setting down to her goal weight. As she imaged this, she experienced a "sinking sensation." She turned it down by 100 pounds, from 250 to 150. She practiced this imagery every day for a week.

There were three things she described which indicated we might very well be onto something new and exciting. One, "I feel fat. I feel like I am jiggling down the hall as I walk and I hate it." Two, "I don't know how to describe it, but I feel uncomfortable, like there is some internal conflict going on." Three, "I went out to Restaurant X, a smorgasbord, with my husband. I was very tired and I knew I would pig out. I always do. But I didn't. I ate a little salad and a spoonful of mashed potatoes. The food just was not very appealing."

One thing that seems to have happened with J.P. is that her perception and experience of herself changed because of imagery. She experienced herself as "fat." One may say, "Of course! She is 100 pounds fat." But she had been fat for over eight years, and this feeling was different. She experienced her body as it truly was, and this was uncomfortable. This change along with her feelings of internal conflict seem reasonable to expect if imagery did, in fact, change her natural biological set point by 100 pounds. She created a huge discrepancy between what should now be her natural weight of 150 and the reality of her 250 pounds. The grand mistake we made was in creating such a great discrepancy, because it resulted in discomfort that proved too much to live with on a constant basis. No, she did not commit suicide. She quit doing the imagery. This is why I now recommend imagining changing set point by 5 to 10 pounds at a time, gradually progressing to the ideal weight.

This approach seemed to have appeared to me out of the blue, but it did not. The conceptual basis for the cellular-imagery approach to weight loss has its foundations borrowed from the fields of psychosomatic medicine and biofeedback. The pioneers in the field of cellular imagery are the researchers and practitioners in the field of biofeedback and some courageous medical doctors, Elmer and Alyce Green, Judith Green, Barbara Brown, Jeanne Achterberg, G. Frank Lawlis, O. Carl Simonton, and Bernie Siegel, to name but a few. Most of the work has been related to treating disease.

How does imagery work? It appears that the mind "activates" or strengthens natural body function through imagery and language. That is, the body process we are imagining is an ordinary, everyday kind of natural happening, whether it be the T-cells of the immune system destroying cancer cells or burning fat to provide energy. The quality of the thought apparently influences the process by activating, strengthening, or suppressing the function.

For example, imagery has and is being used in conjunction with traditional treatment to help patients maximize their bodily defenses against cancer. The quality of imagery has been shown to predict the outcome of the treatment. For example, if the image of cancer is symbolically negative, the outcome tends to be negative. Simonton pointed out that representing cancer cells as ants is a negative symbol. "Have you ever been able to get rid of the ants at a picnic?"

If imagery is technically or medically incorrect, the patient is advised to revise the image. To imagine cancer cells as large, insurmountable boulders is to misrepresent the cancer, for the cells are actually quite weak and easily destroyed by a healthy immune system. Imagery should reflect the fact that cancer cells are weak and the treatment and immune system are strong.

Fear and misunderstanding perpetuate and stimulate negative, inaccurate imagery. The point is that the imagery is used to stimulate an existing natural body process to function more effectively and efficiently. When you imagine your body releasing fat from the fat cells and burning fat for energy, you are merely stimulating processes that happen anyway. You are just doing it better. Your mind is the director of the action.

This is a rather new area of study and the need for further research is evident. However, for hundreds of years, humans knew through their own experience that positive thinking, belief, attitude, etc. resulted in positive results. Albert Schweitzer expressed humility and respect for the innate capabilities of the mind and body when he stated, "It is supposed to be a secret, but I'll tell you anyway. We doctors do nothing; we only help and encourage the doctor within."

However, as faith in the scientific method grew, we began to devalue and mistrust our own experience because we could not "prove it." Certainly, validation of experience is important, and now our technological sophistication has progressed to the point that we can now validate some of the things we knew all along. We can easily tout our expertise and knowledge, but we know very little about the mysteries of life. Despite our naivete and ignorance, the leads are fascinating, and to lose out on the benefits of the gifts of the mind while we wait for the scientific facts would be tragic. Simply put, my personal experiences along with my experiences with my clients, students, and my research have led me to the belief that imagery works. With all honestly, I have not a clue *how* it works. I would love to know the answers to this mystery but, until I do, I will gratefully apply what I know.

As far as I know at this time, no one else has done research of this nature specifically related to weight loss or metabolism. Despite the limited research, you might keep in mind that the conceptual basis is sound. Further, my experience, my clients' experiences, and my rather limited research indicate that imagery changes physiology—that imagining changes in set point, changes in secretions of selected hormones, etc. significantly changes metabolism.

Also, perception of food changes. For example, one lady who participated in the study on the effects of guided imagery on metabolism reported that she always ate as soon as she got home from work. Since she had been practicing the imagery, she said, "I can hardly wait for this study to be over. I don't want to eat after work anymore, but you said we were not supposed to change eating habits until the experiment is over. So I force myself to eat even though I don't want too."

We will begin with an imagery exercise which is very much like the one the people used during my research. Even those individuals who were skeptical at the beginning of the study managed to increase their basal metabolic rate, BMR, the number of calories burned at rest. Chapter 8, "The Personal Power Pack," includes a compendium of these images to which you may refer, picking the ones you wish to work with.

It will be helpful to read "Introduction to Specifics," pages 141-143, before doing Exercise Five.

EXERCISE FIVE

"Burning Fat." Assume a comfortable resting position in a quiet place where you will not be interrupted. Have colored pencils, a pen and your journal near you so you can record your experience immediately following the exercise. Take your time. Relax and "feel" your body. Beginning at your forehead, working down to your toes, become aware of each body part and release any tension, allowing relaxation to spread throughout your body with the awareness. Take a moment and rest in your relaxation, focusing on your breath.

In your imagination, climb into your body and look around. In your imagination, you can do anything and go anywhere. Take a little scenic trip through your body and look at the muscles, the heart . . . what else

Continued →

Exercise Five—cont'd.

can you see? Can you see the storage tanks of reserved fuel, the fat cells?

The fuel in these tanks is not static. It moves freely in and out of the cells. Can you see this fuel circulating? It can travel around in the blood and go where energy is needed. Imagine, in any way that you wish, this fat energy being transformed into other forms of energy, heat, and mechanical energy. "Burning" fat merely means that fat is being transformed. The "burning" is not destructive as fire is destructive. When you are burning fat, you feel warmer because of the heat energy being released. Take your time. There is no hurry.

Are you seeing colors? Do you have a sense of where you are in your body, of movement, of heat? Do you hear anything? Smell anything?

Now, move up into your brain to a very special place called the hypothalamus. It isn't a very big place, but it is very important, for it regulates much of what goes on in the body. Some of the things it regulates are appetite, hunger, and body weight. Imagine in anyway that you wish turning down your set point. This is like "setting" your biological thermostat for body weight to what you want it to be. Set the controls for an exact amount . . . an exact amount five to ten pounds closer to your ideal weight. Be certain that you turn it DOWN. This will automatically decrease your appetite and hunger. This will automatically increase the number of calories you burn.

If you want, you may also turn up a setting which

Continued →

Exercise Five—cont'd.

controls the number of calories you burn. But remember, this is different from the set point, which should be turned down *unless* you want to gain weight.

Now, move directly from the hypothalamus into a small lobular gland which hangs from a stalk. This gland is the pituitary gland which secretes a hormone called Growth Hormone (GH). The hormone is released directly into the blood stream. This wonderful substance makes it possible for children to grow. But for adults, it works a bit differently. It increases the rate at which you burn calories. The more GH, the more fat is burned. It can also help with tissue repair if you are injured, and it can increase the size of your muscles—if and only if you work with weight training. Imagine the pituitary gland releasing more Growth Hormone. See the hormone circulating and acting on the areas of the body which need to release and burn fat. Take your time. Notice what is happening and how. What do you see, feel, and hear?

Then move into your neck to the thyroid gland. Imagine the thyroid gland secreting thyroxine. Thyroxine works much like Growth Hormone. Imagine thyroxine being released right into the blood stream and increasing the fat burned. See and feel it going to the parts of the body which need the most work.

Now imagine the number of furnaces which are needed to transform energy increasing. Not only is the number increasing, but they are also getting bigger. The greater the number and size of the furnaces, the more fuel can be burned. Notice the furnaces

Continued →

Exercise Five—cont'd.

the more fuel can be burned. Notice the furnaces work very well and can burn great quantities of fat. The furnaces are called mitochondria. When we exercise, the number and size of the mitochondria increase. Now the number and size will increase because the mind has directed the body to build and use more furnaces.

Take your time and enjoy the process. Know that each of these thought images acts to change your physiology. Burning fat is a natural process. You are merely burning it faster and you are directing the location of the action.

Lastly, imagine, in any way you wish, your body burning fat and getting leaner naturally. When you open your eyes you know that your body is regulated to approach and maintain its ideal weight. Each image is a gift you have given your body . . . thank your body for responding quickly and expertly to your directions.

Slowly and gently open your eyes and stretch.

EXERCISE SIX

Recording Your Imagery. This exercise is important because it serves as your baseline from which your can compare other imagery experience and see your progress. In your journal, write a brief response describing how you felt about this experience. Sketch as many images as you can remember using colored pencils. Now, answer these questions.

1. Was it easy? Or was it frustrating?

2. Were your images vivid? Were your images colorful?

3. What did you see? Hear? Feel? Smell? Taste? Did you feel yourself moving through your body? Did you feel a change in temperature, your body getting warmer?

4. Did you feel like you were actually in your body, or were you more of an observer (associated or dissociated imagery)?

5. Did you feel uncomfortable with any of the language used in the directions? If so, go back and change the word or wording while preserving the essence of meaning.

6. What parts of the imagery exercise, if any, just did not happen?

7. Did you "do" the exercise without judgment, or were you analyzing it as you tried to follow the directions?

Explanation of Exercise Five: Burning Fat

What part of this exercise has the greatest effect? The fact is that this is unknown. The *only* thing measured scientifically to this point is metabolism . . . which does increase (Kirk, 1988). Metabolism increased significantly from the measurement before to after listening to the cassette tape of guided imagery. The tape was 11 minutes long. Some people increased 200 calories, some as much as 600 calories.

Even more remarkable, however, was that a few people's *baseline* metabolisms increased. That is, their metabolism increased significantly from the first time before they had ever listened to the tape to the second time they were measured *before* listening to the tape. This was a result of practicing with the tape twice a day for six weeks. This is, of course, what we would like to happen for everyone with below-normal metabolic rates . . . for their baselines to be heightened and stay there whether they listen to a tape or not.

When one woman, Mrs. H., saw her first measurement, she said, "I don't know whether to laugh or cry. I know why it has always been so hard for me to lose weight now. I don't need to feel guilty about it anymore. But what can I do about it?"

This woman was much like many of the people in the study who had very low BMRs (about 700 calories per day instead of a more normal 1200 calories, for females). Mrs. H did something, though, because she was one of the subjects who increased her baseline by 600 calories! About six months later, we measured her again. Since she had been ill, she had not continued with the tape or imagery, but her baseline BMR was still 400 calories greater than before practicing imagery.

Hormones and mitochondria have not been measured yet. Hopefully, this will happen soon. When developing this program, I tried to include anything that might work. As with cancer-imagery work, I am working under the similar assumption that specific imagery will enhance the power of the imagery. So far, so good, but certainly there will be refinements in the future as our knowledge base grows.

Now, to address your experience. Much of this explanation will be expanded upon in the next chapter on "Assets and Liabilities." Read through what you have written for Exercise Six before reading the next chapter to refresh your memory. This serves as your "baseline" measurement.

(The numbered items in italics refer back to Exercise Six.)

1. Was it easy? Was it frustrating?

Imagery is a skill. For some it comes naturally and effortlessly. These people describe very vivid, colorful, flashy experiences. In workshops, upon hearing these descriptions, invariably some participant will exclaim in an exasperated tone, "That's wonderful, but *nothing* happened with me!"

I realize your frustration. If you are not one of those fortunate imagers, be patient and know with confidence that it will happen with practice. Practice means setting up the time and opportunity to do the exercises rather than trying harder while you are doing the exercise. Relax and surrender to the suggestions. Trying harder only gets in the way. Remember also that imagery may consist of any one of, or combination of, the senses. You may have wonderful kinesthetic sense (movement, temperature, tactile sensations, emotion) while being "image blind." Imagery can still work for you.

Explanation of Exercises 2 through 4 and 6

The more senses involved, the more effective the imagery.

Involvement and the complexity of the involvement will increase with practice. One of the women in the study reported that she imagined seeing the pictures of the glands she had seen in the instruction booklet the first two times she listened to the tape (dissociated imagery). By the third session, she was happily traveling about the body changing controls and burning fat (associated imagery). The improvement happened naturally and without effort.

5. Did you feel uncomfortable with any of the language used in the directions?

One woman did not like the term "Growth Hormone" because she said that it meant "to get bigger." That is exactly the opposite of what she wanted. Growth Hormone will not make an adult "grow" in the sense that she meant. If understanding this does not change what I call the "cringe response," then merely change the wording. She could use the word "hormone" instead of Growth Hormone.

One of the instructions for relaxation induction asked the listener to count backwards from 10 to 0. The narrator counted 3 . . . 2 . . . 1 . . . 0. One man hated it when the narrator said "zero." No reason, just a gut reaction. In his case, change "zero" to "oh." This is a chance for you to be a creative script writer.

A few people thought it stupid to thank the body for responding. "It's my body and it will do what I want . . . I don't have to 'ask' it to do anything." I disagree, but if that is your position, eliminate the phrase. I included it because I think it is absolutely vital that we appreciate the body. We need to learn to love it. Like nature, it is not something to be conquered and subdued, but rather something to be cherished and to work with cooperatively. The body is not an adversary. Thanking it is a symbolic gesture of respect.

7. *Did you "do" the exercise without judgment, or were you analyzing it as you tried to follow the directions?*

It is pretty difficult not to judge an exercise the first time through. One tends to listen rather than "do," if for no other reason than to know what is coming next. Plus, this is suggestion, and it is powerful. It is a responsible idea to learn what the suggestion is before subjecting yourself to it. But after the initial judgment and analysis, do as Rico recommended and put the judge on the chair besides you and do the exercise. Judgment comes later.

I have only had one person drop out of a program because of the inability to suspend judgment. There are many people whose primary intellectual preference is analytical. Suspending judgment for a prescribed period of time will be more difficult for them. However, do not make the common mistake of confusing difficult with impossible.

Appendix B contains examples with some explanation of imagery described by clients and workshop participants. Sharing imagery experience is important because these experiences serve as suggestions and ideas which work on a subconscious level. Imagery experience becomes richer just by knowing other possibilities and affirming that imagery is a fun thing to do.

Our culture tends to denigrate and devalue the importance of fantasy and dreaming. The denigration has had its effect. People come to invalidate their own internal experience or ignore it. I thank my wonderfully imaginative father for celebrating imagery.

The tradition in our family was to share dreams at

the breakfast table. To be a valued member of this conversation, a kid had to remember the dream. As a result, I became an expert at remembering my dreams just because they were valued, or rather *I* was valued for sharing the experience. I even remembering making a few of them up!

I wanted to have exciting dreams of the wolf-boy and golfing with Ike just like my father. This is why imagery is very easy for me as an adult. If you are a parent, try sharing dreams as a way to facilitate the imagery skill development in your children. It's great fun, too.

Nutritional Imagery

Nutritional imagery is one of the quickest methods to change perception and the meaning of food. This is the way to truly want what you need and give up poor food choices without a sense of sacrifice and deprivation. You will not be tempted by something you do not want.

To do nutritional imagery, we need to know why poor food choices are poor beyond the typical kind of superficial knowledge, "I shouldn't have that 'cause it's fattening." And we need to know the opposite. Why are certain food choices good choices? We need to know what is happening in the body and, when we imagine what is happening, it becomes dramatically real.

The worst general food choice one can make is one that is high in fat content. One gram of fat contains nine calories, more than twice that of carbohydrate and protein, each with four calories per gram. Adding butter and sour cream to a baked potato doubles, triples, or even quadruples caloric intake. The garnishes end up being three times the caloric value of the potato! So butter and sour cream are unwise choices for anyone wishing to decrease body weight. However, the common perception, further reinforced with self-talk, is that the butter and sour cream are "good." Therefore, giving up butter and sour cream are sacrifices.

Statements such as, "Besides, some of my friends eat this stuff and don't gain an ounce. It's not fair," reflect perception and self-talk that literally sets you up for failure. You are only perceiving "good" at the level of taste. In the body, it is absolutely a different story, and the story is similar whether you are skinny or fat. At this level, skinny people do not necessarily have an advantage.

EXERCISE SEVEN

Southern Fried Chicken. You need not do a relaxation induction for this. Merely imagine as you read. This is negative imagery, so make certain that you are imagining this as if it is happening to someone else, not yourself.

You walk into a restaurant and notice a family sitting next to you eating fried chicken and mashed potatoes and gravy. Focus on one person and watch that person chew and swallow. For purposes of example, let us say it is Dad, a 42-year-old bus driver.

"See" the food slide down into his stomach. Since fat takes a long time to digest, the blood must be diverted to the intestines to handle the workload. Dad is going to feel drowsy after this meal. As the fat is absorbed into the circulatory system, the elements of the blood get sticky and clump together. Red blood cells can only go through the smallest vessels in the system, the capillaries, one at a time. Since the red

Continued →

Exercise Seven—cont'd.

blood cells are sticking together, they cannot get through. Up to 20 percent of Dad's capillary beds will close down, which means that the tissues these capillaries supply get very little oxygen. It is like a traffic jam during rush hour. Dad is not only drowsy, he gets sluggish, too. His mental and physical performance will diminish.

The high levels of saturated fat and cholesterol traveling through his system add to the already significant obstruction in the blood vessels. The process of artherosclerosis (hardening of the arteries) continues at an accelerated rate as cholesterol forms plaque deposits in the walls of the vessels. This process started when Dad was a child. The plaque resembles stalagmites and stalactites in caves. The vessels are becoming inflexible, and Dad is now more susceptible to stroke and heart attack.

The fat decreases the movement of the contents of the intestine. It will take up to three days to process this meal. The prolonged period of time the fat stays in the large intestine allows bacteria to produce carcinogenic substances, which increase Dad's risk of colon and prostate cancer.

Although Dad won't be hungry for quite some time, the meal supplies 1600 calories—too much for his sedentary lifestyle. He reasons that he will skip supper. He frequently misses breakfast and works through lunch. His body responds by changing the enzymes in his mitochondria and slows his metabolism. Although he eats fewer calories per day

Continued →

> **Exercise Seven—cont'd.**
>
> by skipping meals, he also burns fewer calories. The excess fat finally finds its way to his already expanding middle.

Explanation of Exercise Seven

This is not aversion therapy, because these images reflect reality. Imagining chocolate chips as bugs in cookies may work for a little while, but it isn't real and the "thinker" knows it. Why not base behavior on reality rather than illusion?

The exercise focuses on only two foods. However, you can work through this example with any food that is high in animal fat. Fat from plant sources is processed differently.

The point is that, as you practice, you will begin to know food beyond the level of taste. The only way to make positive choices consistently is to know everything you can about the choice. So, as you read nutritional material, do more than read. Imagine. Then apply. Once you learn which foods are high in fat, you are well on your way to making better decisions. The more you play with nutritional imagery, the faster your perception will change. Anytime you see someone eating fatty food, play with this imagery.

You will get to a point where you will no longer need to do nutritional imagery. You just will not want fatty foods. You will likely have experiences similar to a former client. A professional man, A., told me how he dreaded going to a dinner meeting because there would not be anything he could eat. Later and excitedly, he told me that he ordered salami and a salad. Even though he was aware of the high fat content, he chose salami because of the special love he had for it.

"But a strange thing happened. As I was eating my salad and looking at the salami, these white flecks stared up at me and YUCK! I just couldn't put that stuff in my body."

His perception surprised him. This experience represents a milestone, because he was no longer struggling to behave as he should. The appropriate choice was automatic.

You must learn which foods are high in fat. There is no need to memorize calories. Jane Brody's *Nutrition Book* (1987) has an excellent chapter on dietary fat, and the author presents the material in an easily understandable fashion. Another way to quickly assess fat content is by calculating the percent of fat from the label on the food container. Instead of comparing grams of fat to grams of protein and carbohydrate (CHO), determine the *percentage* of the total number of calories coming from fat.

For example, suppose a "health" protein-bar label reads: CHO 20 g., Protein 10 g., and Fat 9 g. The bar equals 20 x 4 (CHO) plus 10 x 4 (protein) plus 9 x 9 (fat) = 80 + 40 + 81 = 201 calories. On the surface, 9 grams of fat doesn't look too bad, but you discover that 40 per cent of the calories of the bar come from fat. That is too high.

Although the American Heart Association and the U.S. Dietary Guidelines recommend a total fat intake of 30 per cent, that is too high for a weight-loss program and too high to reverse the vascular disease process. I recommend no more than a 20-per-cent intake for weight loss and, if you can manage it, 10 per cent to reverse vascular disease. Ten percent will require major, challenging dietary modifications for most Americans.

EXERCISE EIGHT

Associated Nutritional Imagery. This exercise is practiced while you are acting out a good choice.

Before you eat, imagine your goal and know that this food choice is a step toward that goal along with all of its associated benefits. Savor the food as you eat and imagine it going down into your body and dispersing to nourish all of your cells. Because the food is packed densely with a variety of nutrients (vitamins, minerals, amino acids), it vitalizes each and every cell of your body, making them strong and healthy.

The elements of your blood flow freely through clean, smooth vessels. Food also moves quickly through the digestive system. If you have had a history of high fat intake, the vascular disease process is reversed . . . you feel more alert, energetic, light and alive.

EXERCISE NINE

"Zipping Imagery." I suppose this could be interpreted as a pornographic exercise, but that is not the imagery I had in mind! Zipping means *quick* imagery. As your skills with imagery improve, you can practice bits and pieces of imagery scenarios anywhere at any time. Zip into the hypothalamus and check your check point. Secrete hormones during a workout . . . you might as well think about supplementing your workouts with thoughts of metabolism and goals instead of thoughts of work at the office. As long as the outcome of the imagery is positive, do associated imagery. If the outcome is negative as with Dad in the chicken example in Exercise Seven, ALWAYS DO DISSOCIATED IMAGERY, with the object of the imagery someone other than yourself. You may wish to create a kind of "generic" person which represents an accurate model of human functioning for this purpose if you are uncomfortable practicing "on a real person."

Application

Imagery works, but it only works when you use it. In the beginning, it is extremely important to systematically include it as part of your day. You are working to overcome old habit patterns. Imagery is suggestion and can therefore easily be included in the program you develop for yourself along with affirmations and goal statements. If you found the exercises difficult, relaxation is a critical element of your program. Choose any of the exercises to use as scripts for a tape and any combination of images found in the "Personal Power Pack." The next chapter will assist you with increasing the effectiveness of your imagery, and Appendix B may give you other suggestions.

Suggested Reading:

Bailey, Covert. *Fit or Fat*. Boston: Houghton Mifflin Co., 1978.

Brody, Jane. *The Jane Brody Nutrition Book*. New York: Bantam Books, 1987.

Garfield, Charles and Bennett, Hal Zina. *Peak Performance*. Los Angeles: Jeremy P. Tarcher, Inc., 1984.

Kirk, Constance C. The effects of guided imagery on basal metabolic rate. *Journal of the Society for Accelerated Leaning and Teaching*. 13(4), 1988, p. 347-361.

Ornish, Dean. *Reversing Heart Disease*. New York: Ballantine Books, 1990.

Pritikin, Ilene and Pritikin, Nathan. *The Official Guide to*

Restaurant Eating. Berkeley: Berkeley Publications, 1985.

Pritikin, Nathan. *The Pritikin Promise.* Berkeley: Berkeley Publications, 1985.

_____*The Pritikin Permanent Weight-Loss Manual.* New York: Bantam Books, 1981.

_____*The Pritikin Program for Diet and Exercise.* New York: Bantam Books, 1979.

Rico, Gabriele Lusser. *Writing the Natural Way.* Los Angeles: J.P. Tarcher, Inc., 1983.

Walford, Roy L. *The 120 Year Diet.* New York: Simon and Schuster, 1986.

Whitaker, Julian M. *Reversing Heart Disease.* New York: Warner Books, 1985.

• 7 •

Assets & Liabilities: Enhancing the Power of Imagery

People are not created equal. They vary in preference, talent, and ability. Variations of preference, talent, and ability are just as great in the area of imagery as in other areas of endeavor. Some people seem to be endowed with natural ability. Or perhaps they were fortunate enough to have their creative abilities nurtured directly or indirectly. Others have to work at it.

The good news is that imagery, being a primary way that humans think, is a *natural* ability. If we let it, it will develop just as naturally and effortlessly as language.

The challenge comes in trying to shape imagery to suit our needs and yield a desired outcome. To do this, we attempt to pattern our imagery from the character-istics found to be common in successful people. Most of the characteristics of successful imagery can be learned.

Surrender Versus Effort

> To "have" running water you must let go of it
> and let it run.
>
> —Alan Watts

Albert Einstein said he did not get ideas. They "got" him. Michael Jackson says the tunes he writes are not his but come "through" him. Both these people exemplify a receptive attitude. The creators must allow the ideas and tunes to come to them. In effect, ego, self-criticism, negative emotions, and even desire must get out of the way for these gifts to be received.

The clients and people who served as volunteers for research with metabolism all wanted imagery to work. Some were downright desperate. A few of these people wanted the goal so badly that they enacted with a vengeance the message they received in childhood, "If you want something bad enough, all you have to do is work hard to get it."

This maxim works for many goals, but it is one of the most serious and common barriers to effective imagery. The definition of effort as it relates to imagery must be changed. Effort is planning and systematically carrying out reading, learning, and times for practice. During practice, one needs to let go and surrender.

It is much easier to call a dog and let him run to you than it is to chase him. The more you pursue him, the more likely he is to elude and tease you with a "run circles around the foolish master" game. Some "master!" Images are like the dog. We can call the images through suggestion (guided imagery, fantasy, and affirmations) rather than through "trying hard." Trust and allow images from the right hemisphere of the brain to come to you. Pursuit only leads to failure and frustration.

How does one surrender? This unfamiliar territory is a bit frightening because it seems to contradict the need to be in control. There are two ways to foster surrender. One, suggest to yourself that it is perfectly okay to suspend control and effort for this short practice period. Let the right brain have its way with you, knowing full well that this cannot harm you in any way, that it is temporary, that you can intervene at any time, that you are in control of the time frame and the environment, and judgment and analysis will come when you are finished.

Two, include a systematic relaxation induction/technique at the beginning of your program. This is especially important for countering the effort syndrome.

I ran into one of my former clients at a movie theater about six months after she completed one of the ten-week Weight Dynamics[1] group sessions. With great elation, she thanked me and said she had lost 26 pounds and felt wonderful. We visited together privately the last week of the session because she was frustrated with her lack of progress. She clearly conveyed desire and determination. However, the desire and determination were being converted into effort. She was, in fact, creating a barrier. Once she understood this, she was able to choose to take a more passive attitude while actually practicing the techniques, and then she easily met her goal.

One of the surest ways to know if you are adequately surrendering and relaxing is by your images. Under the best conditions, images will come freely and easily as if they have a life of their own. Many times the images will surprise you. You do not know where they came from, but in retrospect you might figure out the origin of some of the content. One woman described an image to control chocolate craving. "The Smurfs"™ would go down into her stomach and spray the lining of the stomach with chocolate mist. This totally eliminated the craving. Why Smurfs? Her grandchildren loved the Smurfs. Her association and familiarity with them made them available and her right brain put them to work. This is an example of a totally creative solution which came to her without effort.

A 15-year-old client was using a cassette tape with imagery for changing metabolism for several weeks. Each week I would ask her about the imagery work and she would reply that she was working with it. No big deal. Nothing flashy here. Then one day she literally bubbled with enthusiasm and excitement.

"I came home from school, put the tape on, and lay down on the bed. I was really tired. It was so different. I was actually in my body traveling around, and I could see everything!" Now she was actually experiencing imagery. The images were not contrived. They just happened, and they happened with unbelievable clarity. She was persistent in setting up the opportunity for imagery to occur by patiently listening to the tape time after time. That was the effort. Finally, when she was relaxed enough, the imagery came to her. Perhaps, if relaxation techniques don't work for you, you should try this girl's technique—fatigue!

Positive Expectation Versus Negative Expectation

There are reams of research validating the inherent power held in one's expectations. It ranges from the first and classic "Pygmalion effect" studies on classroom and work-related performance to the effect of expectation on the outcome of cancer treatment. Results consistently support the hypothesis that expectation is a self-fulfilling prophecy. Expectation can work just as powerfully in a negative as in a positive form. If you hold an image in your mind, that energy is somehow transformed into its physical equivalent. Therefore, if you expect to succeed, you will; if you expect to fail, you will.

A client, T.K., was nervous about going home to Nebraska for Thanksgiving. She was progressing very well on the program, feeling good about herself and the weight she was losing. To counter feelings of anxiety and to ensure continued success, she practiced mental rehearsal. She envisioned herself being home with her family and friends, enjoying the company, making appropriate food choices, and feeling good about herself for her positive choices rather than feeling deprived. One evening when she expressed reservations about the impending trip home, I asked if she had been practicing the mental rehearsal frequently. She said, "Oh yes. I see myself doing and feeling all the right things. But I just know when I get home it will be like it always is. I'll give up and eat like everyone else."

The last statement indicated that she was actively undermining all the practice she was doing with negative expectation. She expected to fail. Mental rehearsal should help change negative expectation. In T.K.'s case, she was not aware of this form of negativity. The best cure for negative expectation is to experience success. When you fail once, you will naturally think of failure when the situation or challenge presents itself again. Use imagery and language to counter. Use language as the form of suggestion to affirm the possibility of positive outcome of imagery.

Belief and Faith

No one is ready for a thing until he believes
he can acquire it.
                              —Napoleon Hill

There is an obvious relationship between Hill's statement and expectation. Belief and faith influence expectation. Cancer patients who had faith—whether it be faith
in God, themselves, or the future—had better treatment
outcome than those patients who did not. Also, people
who have internal locus of control (meaning that they
believe they influence the quality and content of their
lives) have better treatment outcome than people who
have external locus of control. (External locus means that
one believes the control over one's life is governed by
some external power such as fate, the stars, the boss, etc.)

If you have worked with the exercises, you know
now that you have at least some internal locus of control.
You control the direction of your thoughts, and these
thoughts in turn influence your very physiology. So,
through your practice, you should have automatically
increased your faith factor.

It is natural to resist new, innovative information
because to accept the new we must give up obsolete
ideas and information. We have to change. The change is
sometimes frightening because it involves risk.

There are two ways to approach the problem of resistance. One is to image giving up the old and useless with
a sense of joy in receiving new, challenging information
and experience. The second is through autosuggestion.
Hill stated, "Repetition of affirmation of orders to your
subconscious mind is the only known method of voluntary development of the emotion faith." The heartening
thing about Hill's ideas is that faith, just as with other

elements needed for effective imagery, can be developed with the skill and technique of autosuggestion.

Self-Love Versus Self-Hate

A basic underlying assumption I have concerning behavior is that one must care, love, and respect oneself before long-lasting, life-affirming change can occur. People will not nurture what they don't like and love, at least not for long. This nurturing applies to the self as well. Everything presented in this book requires an investment of time and commitment geared toward helping yourself. If you hate yourself, your personal law is that you are worthless or despicable and certainly not worthy of investment. Further, you are not worthy of success.

You may be conscious or unconscious of this belief. If self-loathing is unconscious, you may progress toward your goal and then, to your own surprise and bewilderment, sabotage your success. Sabotage will be a recurrent life pattern perpetuating anger, hostility, and frustration. If self-hate is conscious, you are empowered with that awareness. If you lack self-worth, you need to work with affirmations, imagery, and faith directed specifically to this problem. This is the most important work you will ever do. I encourage anyone who finds this process difficult, painful, or frightening to seek professional counseling. There are times when we need someone else's eyes to help us "see," to open our own awareness, which is often clouded by repression, reaction formation, denial, etc.

A prevalent misconception is that taking care of and nurturing oneself is selfish. However, there is a tremendous amount of evidence which validates the destructive effects of self-hate. People share what they have and what they know. Those who know only self-hate give it to others in the form of violence and disease. Self-hate is extremely costly economically. Even more tragic is the loss of human potential. Those who know self-love give their love to others. Nurturing yourself will ultimately nurture others and the earth.

Specialized Knowledge Versus Ignorance

Learn as much as you can about nutrition and the way your body and mind function. Incorporate what you learn into your imagery and behavior. New knowledge and different perspectives can help maintain your enthusiasm and excitement. Choice and decision should be made on the basis of information integrated with ideals and personal goals. Blind action leads to erratic and dangerous consequences. Action has consequence. Always ask, "What are the potential consequences? Can I live happily with those consequences?"

Specifics of Imagery

It is believed that at least three aspects of the five senses are involved in successful imagery. Figures A and B are imagery sketches done by the same person. The imagery is very rich, for it involves color, movement, sound, and vivid visual representation. By the way, this person was very successful with losing and maintaining her weight. The process was easy for her. She enjoyed imagery a great deal.

However, imagery can be successful with fewer aspects. The person who drew figure C did not see anything, but she could represent it pictorially and she felt it. Some of the subjects in the metabolic study had what would be considered poor imagery . . . it lacked detail,

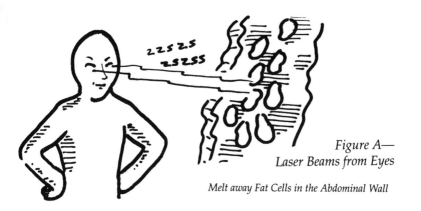

Figure A—
Laser Beams from Eyes

Melt away Fat Cells in the Abdominal Wall

Figure B—
Self Turning on the Pituitary

Figure C—Shower of Growth Hormone

strength, etc., but they were still successful with increasing metabolism. Trying too hard and the exclusive use of language over imagery proved to be greater obstacles than the richness of the imagery.

Refer back to Exercise Five ("Burn Fat") in the last chapter. How many senses were represented? There is no need to judge yourself too harshly. Remember that different people have different abilities and preferences.

Wherever you have begun, you can improve even if you are a hot shot. One way is through suggestion.

Select an exercise you enjoyed. Determine which sense you need and want to experience, one that does not ordinarily occur for you. Before you even begin the relaxation induction, say to yourself, "This time there will be sound [or whatever you wish]." Give the suggestion with positive conviction, without signs of doubt. Be emphatic and totally positive just as you would with an affirmation. There are any number of things you might suggest—sound, temperature, movement, vividness and clarity, strength, etc. Once you have mastered one, the others will come more readily.

The suggestion is given before the relaxation induction because relaxation alters consciousness. Once relaxed, as brain waves slow and change from beta to alpha, suggestion is difficult. That is why it is easier to listen to a tape than to do imagery exercise on your own. Certain cognitive abilities are only available to us in specific states of consciousness. You know this through experience. For example, one cannot talk reasonably with an angry person. Anger is a state of consciousness that obstructs the ability to communicate. Even if the angry person wanted to talk, she couldn't. Likewise, if I want to fly or solve a problem in my dreams, I must give the suggestion before I sleep or dream. Suggestion is a cognitive ability available to me in waking consciousness but not in dreaming and sleep consciousness. The mind then works with the suggestion as if it carried the suggestion from one state of consciousness to another state. It may take several times for the suggestion to work.

Another way to enhance the richness of imagery is to share your imagery experience. Refer to Appendix B. Practice the exercises with a friend or a group of friends.

Another way is to just quit trying and work with what you have. As you relax into the exercises and play with imagery, you will improve.

Symbolism: Effective imagery tends to be symbolic rather than concrete. Cancer patients envision Pac-Man™ characters eating cancer "gremlins." Mounted knights ride through the body seeking and destroying cancer cells. The knight is a powerful image of good and purity. Weight-loss images include burning fat in furnaces or with torches, Pac-Man eating fat cells, fat melting away like snow melting into a river, and fat cells bursting like balloons.

It is important that the image is congruent with one's value system. Some people feel very uncomfortable using caustic, destructive images. Elizabeth Kübler-Ross related a story of a cancer patient she was working with who would not, could not, imagine killing his cancer cells even if they were killing him. He was a Quaker and strictly followed the commandment, "Thou shalt not kill." He came up with his own imagery. Little gnome-like creatures lovingly carried the cancer cells out of his body. As you practice and try some of the imagery coming from the scripts or the examples, play with images. Use ones that feel right and comfortable. Practice writing your own scripts in your own words.

The next chapter, "The Personal Power Pack," offers

a vast array of images and affirmations to help you shorten your scripts. There is just no way to shorten the task enough to satisfy someone like my favorite penguin, Opus of *Bloom County*, who stated, "For goodness sake, I am a typical overweight American . . . and I'd like a diet plan which allows me to remain a lazy pig. Thank you." If you are feeling a bit weary and are tempted to lean toward penguin possibilities, remember the words of Richard Bach: "There is no such thing as a problem without a gift for you in its hands."

Notes

1. "Weight Dynamics" is the registered service trade name I use for seminars and workshops I conduct throughout the country. The workshops range from single presentations to weekly group sessions. Interested parties may contact me through Llewellyn.

• 8 •

The Personal Power Pack: Using Language and Imagery Together

The purpose of the Power Pack is to make weight and body composition control easier. When used properly, it serves as an effective tool for the process of weight loss and maintenance, a process which most people experience as a continuous struggle.

This process need not be a battle when we learn to think in different ways which coordinate volition or will with imagination. Remember, as Emile Coué stated, if the will and imagination are in conflict, imagination always wins. When we get the will and the imagination to work together, the conflict and struggle cease once and for all.

This "Personal Power Pack" is a compilation of affirmations and images. This collection of statements/ images has been generated from research and from many different people; therefore, you must choose the ones that are appropriate for you. It is not my intention for you to use all of them all of the time. The ones that seem to jump out at you, almost as if they were written precisely for you, are the ones to start with. One of the most convenient ways to use them is to write the statements on individual note cards so that you can easily carry them with you as well as add or delete statements as you progress. However, there are many ways to use them. They will be discussed later. First, let us look at exactly what we are attempting to accomplish with the use of the Personal Power Pack.

The Purpose of the Personal Power Pack

Ultimately, *you* will change the way you think about food, eating, weight, your body, and perhaps even your physiological processes through repetition of the affirmations and images. When these thought patterns become habitual ways of thinking, the struggle most dieters experience is diminished or totally eliminated. The note cards merely function as a convenient way to access thoughts you must work on in order to succeed.

Use of the Power Pack will:

1) Stimulate awareness: You are only free to make informed choices if you are aware that choices exist. While eating, you may be thinking about work, the kids, the television program or newspaper you are watching or reading . . . habit takes care of the feeding, habit makes the choice. Until you learn new, more positive habits, you must not trust habit to meet your true needs and wants.

Focusing on an affirmation/ image will direct your attention (will) and stimulate your imagination to create what you need and want. Will and imagination work together rather than in opposition.

2) Reprogram self-talk and self-imagery: Through the years we have all developed habitual patterns or ways of thinking. If the thinking is negative (life-denigrating), then the resulting behavior will usually be destructive. If the thinking is positive (life-affirming), then the outcome will enhance quality of life. We change bad habits by replacing them with good habits. It is not good enough just to say, "Don't think like that." We must learn to redirect thought. Note that we are redirecting the energy of thought rather than trying to constrict or restrain it. The energy *must* manifest . . . we are just choosing the direction of the manifestation.

3) Provide you with a successful history through mental rehearsal: One's confidence increases significantly with success. By practicing "right" behavior over and over again in your mind, you are experiencing success. The subconscious cannot distinguish between real and imaginary scenarios. The purpose is, through practice, to imprint the success image.

4) Influence physiological process: Thought produces physiological responses. Again, by thinking in certain ways, we are choosing the outcome or response. Remember that every one of the participants in the metabolic study I conducted on the effects of guided imagery on basal metabolic rate could increase metabolism in 11 minutes with very little instruction. A few individuals changed their baseline metabolic rates by as much as 600 calories! It seems unbelievable to think that one can merely sit there and think about burning calories and

have it happen, but the fact is that they did. The exact images and affirmations they received via a cassette tape are included here. (Note that this imagery is not meant to replace exercise but to supplement it!)

Research on imagery is in its infancy, especially with regard to metabolism and weight control. The guided images included for increasing metabolism were included based on "best guesses." That is, based on what we know now, it is logical that these mechanisms are involved in the processes. It doesn't seem too scientific, but we do not know all of the mechanisms, hormones, etc. involved in weight control just as we do not know all the immune/healing system mechanisms involved in overcoming cancer. And yet imagery has been shown to be effective in the treatment of cancer and other diseases. So, in an act of faith, we "ask" our bodies through the language and images of the mind to direct body function. We do not need to know exactly *how* it works to know that it *does* work. The body knows how to do it. Of course, we are searching for this knowledge.

There are several parallels which can serve as examples. We have known for centuries that positive thinking has incredible power, but it is just recently that technology has been developed to the point of sophistication and resolution to measure thought energy. Likewise, yogis have been able to control many physiological functions such as heart rate, skin temperature, etc. at will. Now, with biofeedback equipment, everyday, run-of-the-mill non-yogis—i.e., you and me— can do the same thing. Why, even a cross-section of midwest Americana learned how to increase metabolism in about 20 minutes!

5) To coordinate will with imagination: Listen to dieters long enough, in some cases nanoseconds, and you'll hear them talk about food and recipes. Research

has shown that people actually do become physiologically hungry from just thinking about food. Insulin secretion increases, which in turn drops blood-sugar levels, which creates hunger. Advertisers know this and are expert at stimulating images which trigger hunger. By simply and willingly switching the images, you need not trigger hunger or even feelings of deprivation. The affirmation/images help you learn to switch images and language, which results in different, successful responses. And it stands to reason that, if you have enough successful responses, you will obtain and maintain your goal.

How to Use the Personal Power Pack

There are many ways to use this information. Note cards are a convenient, fast way to access what you need when you need it. However, there are other usages.

Read through the entire list and select the affirmations which seem to have been written *for you*. Different people will select different ones based on their unique experiences and needs. The number will vary, too. After you have made your selection, write them on note cards and place them in the order of importance. This order is entirely subjective. Then, depending upon the amount of time and commitment you have, select how many you want to work with each day . . . three to 20. The number will vary, too, depending upon how you choose to work with them. Writing them out 10 to 20 times takes much more time, of course, than listening to them on a tape or reading them.

1) Read through them at least three times a day, especially before meal time. As you read, take the time to dwell on or hold the image or thought in your mind for a few seconds. Other prime reading times are before you

get up in the morning and right before you go to sleep at night.

2) Write them down. Begin with 10 to 20 repetitions in first, second, and third person, twice a day. For example, "I deserve to be successful; I, Connie, deserve to be successful; Connie deserves to be successful." It is thought that the varying forms elicit subtle though different changes in the subconscious mind. Personally, I favor writing affirmations over any other form of usage for several reasons. Writing engages all the dominant senses— vision, hearing, and kinesthetic sense. Writing serves to keep you focused on the task rather than taking mental holidays to who knows where.

Another advantage of writing your affirmations is that you can make changes in wording if you feel any irritation or resistance with the form offered. As a matter of fact, you need to change them if that is the case. You will find that many of the affirmations have similar meanings; the wording varies precisely for the purpose of allowing you a choice. Select the one that is the most comfortable.

Also, writing helps you identify other negatives or barriers which might impede success. As you write, if any negative thought is stimulated by the affirmation, write it down. Symbolically, this represents letting go of the thought. Depending upon the nature of the negative statement, it might indicate other essential affirmations you *must* use to be successful. For example, "I deserve to be successful . . . but my mama always told me I wouldn't amount to a tinker's dam." The negative indicates that, in order to move on with my life, I need to forgive my mama instead of harboring resentment and blame. Quite literally, I have had clients in their 50s and 60s, their parents deceased, who still blame their parents for their conditions and misfortunes. Until they mourn their lost childhoods, forgive, and finally assume adult responsibility, they will remain stuck.

Select four or five of the most important affirmations to work with every day. Write them 10 to 20 times each, twice a day, along with any negatives. After two or three days, you may eliminate the negatives. You know that you have made progress when the affirmation pops into your mind without effort, by itself, at times when it is most important. Then you move to new affirmations. Review the old ones once or twice a week.

Affirmations are extremely powerful when used properly. Most people do not realize this precisely because they quit too soon. Repetition is the key, and *you are not done until the thought or image is automatic even in the most challenging of circumstances.* Prime examples of a challenging circumstances are when you are extremely tired, sick, or are under other kinds of stress. Old thought patterns come back to haunt us during these times. I am not sure we ever entirely get rid of them, but we can certainly make other messages more powerful than the old ones. Again, it takes much repetition. The stronger the old pattern, the more repetitions it will take. Remember, the old ones have had the advantage of years of repetition! If you have a setback, it is not a sign of failure but rather a sign that you need *more* work or *different* work.

3) Imagery, especially that of mental rehearsal and that for affecting physiological process, works best during deep relaxation with some guidance. You can put the choices of images and affirmations on a cassette tape with your favorite music. One advantage of a tape is that you can put a great many images and affirmations on the tape. It is wonderful for reviewing many at once.

Research also shows that we are more suggestible in a deeply relaxed state. Using all forms—writing, reading, and tape resources—should prove to be most beneficial. Since time is such a valuable resource, you must decide which forms you want to use.

Once you know the imagery, you can zap in and out of it in seconds. Whip into the hypothalamus and check the set point, for example. You can do it any time, any place, and frequently. This makes the excuse of "I don't have time" more than a bit flimsy!

Baroque music such as selections from Bach is probably best. "New Age" music, which includes the work of Steve Halpern and George Winston, is also effective. Experiment a bit to find what is the most relaxing and peaceful for you.

Introduction to Specifics of This Imagery/Affirmation Material

It helps to know a little about the territory you are about to enter. Despite the previous introduction, it will be helpful to review this material before proceeding, or review sections of the book. Refer to the next page for diagrams of the hypothalamus, pituitary, and thyroid glands.

The Hypothalamus: The hypothalamus is a specialized area located in the brain which functions to regulate many body processes (e.g., thirst, hunger, appetite, etc.). This is where the "set point" for your body weight is located. In visualization, you will imagine lowering the set point to your goal weight. This, in turn, will increase metabolism (the number of calories you burn). You may think of this like the controls of an air conditioner. You decrease the temperature setting, which increases the energy output to make the house cooler. With set point,

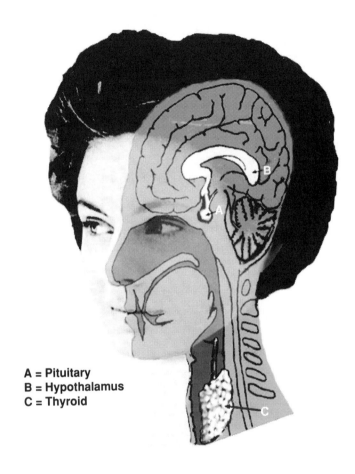

A = Pituitary
B = Hypothalamus
C = Thyroid

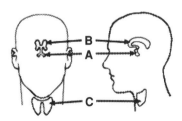

when you decrease the set point, which increases energy output, you should feel your body getting warmer, not cooler.

The Endocrine glands (pituitary and thyroid): Endocrine glands secrete hormones directly into the blood stream. These hormones travel throughout the body to "target" tissues/cells. Wherever the blood travels, the hormones travel as well. For all practical purposes, remember that all body cells have a blood supply.

Growth hormone (GH) from the pituitary gland acts to:

1. increase the rate of protein synthesis in all cells of the body. This is good news if you are working on body composition because it helps build muscle tissue;

2. increase mobilization of fats and use of fats for energy;

3. decrease the rate of carbohydrate utilization by all or most cells.

Thyroxine is secreted from the *thyroid gland* located in the neck. It controls the general rate of metabolism of the body. A total lack of thyroxine production by the thyroid gland decreases the metabolic rate to about half normal. Secretion of very large amounts of thyroxine can increase the rate of metabolism to as much as twice normal. Therefore, overall, the thyroid gland can change the rate of metabolism as much as fourfold.

A person with excess production of thyroxine usually loses weight, sometimes very rapidly. On the other hand, a person with less than normal production of thyroxine often develops extreme obesity.

We are trying to normalize thyroxine levels with these mental exercises. At this point, we do not know if imagery can produce "super-burners."

Now, act!

1. I go into the hypothalamus and adjust the set point to my ideal weight.

The set point is the "thermostat" for your biological weight, or the weight that is natural for you. If the set point is set at your goal weight, it will make your present weight unnatural, and your body will naturally begin to regulate your system so that you will move toward your goal.

Caution: You should lower your set point only 5 to 10 pounds below your current weight, especially if you have a great deal of weight to lose. A great disparity between set point and goal weight may make you feel uncomfortable.

2. I regulate the controls of the hypothalamus to increase the number of calories I burn. I can see the exact number of calories I wish to burn.

It doesn't matter how you choose to do this . . . some people adjust a dial or lever; some punch in the value (number of calories burned per day) into a computer.

Note #1: Set point is turned down. Calorie control is turned up.

Note #2: "Burning" calories just means that you are transforming one kind of energy into another. Therefore, the burning process is not destructive as one might imagine a fire to be.

3. I feel my body getting warmer. This is natural because, when you burn calories, the calories are transformed into heat energy as well as mechanical energy. The warmth you feel is part of this natural process. It is not a "hot" flash, nor is it enough to cause sweating. The warmth is natural and pleasing because it is an indication that what you are doing is working.

Related Affirmations:

a) My set point is _____.

b) My metabolism is naturally high.

c) My body naturally burns excess calories.

d) I am naturally satisfied.

e) My body transforms calories into abundant energy.

f) Good choices are gifts to myself.

If any wording or terminology feels uncomfortable, awkward, or irritating, change it while preserving the essence of meaning.

4. I imagine my pituitary gland secreting abundant amounts of Growth Hormone. The Growth Hormone is a brilliant, powerful color. I imagine it circulating throughout my body; wherever my blood goes, my Growth Hormone goes.

5. I imagine my Growth Hormone interacting with my fat cells to release and transform fat into energy . . . a natural process.

Growth Hormone acts to increase metabolism. It functions to increase the rate at which you burn calories (and fat); it also increases the rate of protein synthesis. If you need to heal tissue from an injury, surgery, or trauma—or build muscle tissue—Growth Hormone is a plus.

As an adult, Growth Hormone will not make you grow bigger (unless we're talking about muscle size, and then you would need to engage in weight training).

Related Affirmations:

a) The amount of Growth Hormone circulating in my system is adequate enough to keep my metabolism naturally high.

b) GH interacts with all my fat cells . . . helping to release and burn fat.

6. I imagine the hormone thyroxine being secreted in abundant amounts from the thyroid gland in my neck. The thyroxine is a brilliant, powerful color. I imagine it mingling with Growth Hormone and circulating throughout my body; wherever my blood goes, thyroxine goes.

7. I imagine my thyroxine interacting with my fat cells to release and transform fat into energy . . . a natural process.

Related Affirmations:

a) My thyroid gland is perfectly healthy.

b) My thyroid gland functions adequately enough to help me achieve and maintain my ideal weight.

8. I imagine moving throughout my body. I can see, hear, and feel my body ridding itself of excess fat.

Related Affirmations:

a) My fat cells are getting smaller and smaller.

b) The large and numerous furnaces within my body burn all excess fat.

There are quite literally furnaces within the cells of the body. These furnaces, called mitochondria, are where food is broken down to release energy. Exercising increases the size and number of mitochondria. That is why exercise is so important in any weight-loss program. It serves to increase metabolism. We are trying to do the same thing here through imagery and languaging. But that is not a reason to neglect exercise!

9. I imagine my hormones acting within and throughout my body to effectively rid my body of excess fat.

This simplifies the other images by combining them. Hormones are messengers which regulate body function.

10. I imagine myself before the mirror. I can see myself looking fit, thin, and strong. I feel healthy—energetic and happy.

11. I imagine myself trying on new clothes, the ones I have always wanted to wear. They slide on easily and effortlessly.

12. I imagine myself doing the activities I want to do easily and effortlessly. Playing and working with ease and with a sense of self-confidence.

Related Affirmations:

a) I will weigh _____ lbs. by _____ (date).

b) I will buy _____ for myself when I reach my goal weight of _____ by _____ (date).

c) I love my body and thank it for responding so quickly to the positive choices I continue to make.

d) I respect my body and demonstrate this respect with gifts of good food choices and exercise.

e) I love the effects of exercise.

f) Exercise is a gift to my body and therefore a gift to myself.

g) I deserve to be successful.

h) Health is my natural state of being.

i) God (My Higher Power) guides me and gives me the strength to make good choices.

If you believe in God or a "Higher Power," incorporating your belief system into your affirmations will enhance the power of the affirmation. Use whatever name or term fits your belief system.

j) Health is a process and I am discovering that I enjoy the process of moving toward my divine right and privilege of perfect health and vitality.

k) I have the power to make my own choices.

l) I reclaim my power to make positive choices.

m) My health is dependent upon my choices. Since I love myself as God loves me, I choose to enact my power of choice.

n) Since I can imagine my goal, I can create my goal.

o) Every positive choice contributes to moving toward my goal.

p) I act now.

q) I choose to act now to achieve my goal.

r) I am responsible for my choices in action and in thought.

As Frances Vaughan states in *The Inward Arc* (1986), most of us know that we are responsible for our actions. But few acknowledge responsibility for their thoughts. Thoughts are the originators of actions. Ultimately, positive thoughts yield positive action; negative thoughts yield negative action.

s) My body is my most precious possession.

13. I imagine myself in an "eating situation." I see, hear, and feel myself going through the situation acting in the way I truly wish to act. I see, hear, and feel myself making choices which move me toward my goal. I feel my self-confidence grow and become stronger. It is easy and natural, free from struggle. There is enjoyment and freedom in making life-affirming decisions.

Always use this exercise before any eating or drinking situation. Repetition is the key to imprinting the image of success. Once the image is imprinted, you will not need the exercise.

14. I imagine interacting with people in eating situations and creatively responding to my own needs. I am not required to explain why I make the choices I do. When someone offers me food that is not a good choice and that I truly do not want, I respond, "No thank you, I don't care for any." Or, "Thank you, no. I am not hungry for that." Or, "It looks wonderful, but I am not hungry for it right now."

You do not need to go into the fact that you're trying to lose weight or that you "shouldn't" or "ought not to" have it. To do so reinforces the act as something against your will . . . this a choice, a free choice which you claim. Every time you exercise free choice, you become stronger.

Related Affirmations:

a) I become stronger with each positive choice I make.

b) I become healthier with each positive choice I make.

c) Making a good choice is an act of freedom.

15. I see people respond to me in positive ways. They acknowledge my success. I am proud of my success because it feels wonderful to be perfectly free and healthy.

16. I imagine myself exercising with joy and ease. I can feel my muscles becoming stronger and more flexible. I can feel my body getting warm, a sign I am responding to exercise in beneficial ways.

Related Affirmations:

a) The physical fatigue of exercise feels good; it signals appropriate body response.

b) My body naturally adapts to exercise by becoming stronger and healthier.

17. I imagine the food I eat and drink nourishing each cell of my body.

18. I imagine food and drink making me stronger and healthier.

It is difficult if not impossible to imagine "junk" food as nourishing. So, make a concentrated effort to imagine this when you are actively engaged with a positive choice. If you are on the verge of making a negative choice, practicing this one BEFORE you decide to eat may be all you need to get you into the "I don't want this" mind-set. This is the most powerful mind-set you can be in because you cannot be tempted to eat something you really don't want. Note that this is *not* an "I shouldn't or ought not eat this" but a true choice based on your desire to nourish your body. You love and respect yourself and your body. Here you can see how the affirmations interconnect. If you hate yourself, then destructive choice is predictable.

Related Affirmations:

a) I savor all I eat and drink.

Food is not the enemy. Food is necessary for providing

nutrients essential for growth, tissue repair, replenishment, and energy. Food is a blessing of life. Savoring does several things:1) It increases one's enjoyment. To savor means you are receiving food as a gift of life. If you believe in God or a Higher Power, this is an excellent time to give thanks and demonstrate your appreciation of the body God gave you through life-affirming choice and action. 2) It slows you down so that you are satisfied with less food. Less food need not mean less enjoyment. It takes approximately 20 minutes for the food you eat to register in the eating regulatory mechanisms for hunger and appetite in the brain. 3) It keeps you "conscious" of *what* you are eating and that you *are*, in fact, eating. It breaks into the program of the fork-to-mouth-to-gut robot. You can only savor those things you are aware of. And, more importantly, there is no responsibility or choice where there is no awareness. Savoring allows for choice. 4) It enhances perception especially if combined with the imagery and affirmation of food nourishing the body. That is, you begin to see and interpret food differently. You give food a new meaning, one of "food as a necessity and a blessing of life, a gift." This is quite different from the battle against food.

b) I choose the meaning I give to food. Food is a gift.

c) Food is a gift of life. I am free to enjoy all kinds of food and drink.

You enjoy good food in abundance. Focus on enjoyment. When and if you reward yourself for whatever reason, build new associations with food. Instead of using "decadent" food as the reward which is the usual association, [refer to the mind-mapping exercise], build new reward systems with good choices such as frozen yogurt instead of ice cream.

Most people have just never considered savoring and

enjoying water! Focus on the hydrating qualities of water. Try bottled water. It may be that you have never tasted good water.

19. I imagine my fat cells getting smaller with each good choice I make.

20. I imagine my blood vessels being clean and smooth.
The cardiovascular disease process is reversible. Plaque build-up (the cholesterol-calcium deposits in and on the vessels) can decrease with exercise and a low fat diet.

21. I imagine the elements of my blood, such as red blood cells, moving freely and easily throughout my vascular system.
A high-fat meal makes the elements of the blood sticky and the red blood cells clump together. Since the red blood cells can only move through the capillaries one cell at a time, single file, about 20 per cent of the capillary beds are closed down just like a traffic jam! Both mental and physical performance diminish as a result. Oxygen and carbon dioxide, along with nutrients etc., make exchanges at the level of the capillaries. Since the tissue's oxygen supply is cut off, it is no wonder you feel sluggish and drowsy after a high-fat meal.
Using other people's negative choice to your advantage:
The point of this kind of practice is that: a) it helps to change your perception of food; b) it helps you regain or maintain your perspective; c) it helps you avoid wallowing in self-pity; d) it provides practice. Imagery is a skill and, therefore, you will get better with practice.

22. I imagine the negative effects poor food choices have on the people eating them.
Instead of lamenting," I don't *get* to have the food other people eat," remember that nobody gets away with

eating bad food. A person may be thin and eat great amounts of junk food. In terms of body weight, he/she is getting away with it. But at the level of performance, at the level of cardiovascular health, and at the level of insulin and blood-sugar response, there is damage. Since they do not have the benefit of your perception and knowledge, they cannot make a choice. They are not free to make a responsible choice. Don't get self-righteous. It is just a matter of a different level of consciousness.

Through the exercises in imagery and languaging, you are internalizing knowledge. You are changing meaning and interpretation of decision and food. You are not the same as the people who *get* to eat anything they want. The only difference is that you *know* and they don't. They have not internalized the knowledge as you have. You are a special person in the sense that you have made the effort to change in a positive way. You have made an excellent investment in your present and your future.

Related Affirmations:

a) Every decision chooses the future.

b) Every decision chooses the present.

23. I can see the fat that people eat go directly to their fat cells for deposit.

24. I can see the fat that people eat make their blood sticky and slow blood flow in their bodies.

25. I can see the fat that people eat coat their blood vessels in plaque—which leads to high blood pressure, stroke, and cardiovascular disease.

Related Affirmations:

a) I choose a different, healthier lifestyle than most other people.

b) I choose positive action for positive consequence.

c) Action yields consequence.

Caution: Never practice negative imagery on yourself.

Using Other People's Positive Choices for Your Benefit

26. I imagine the positive effects of the good food and exercise choices of other people.

27. I can see and feel his/her blood moving freely and easily through the body system.

28. I can see and feel excess fat being burned and transformed into abundant energy.

29. I can see and feel his/her muscles getting stronger, leaner, and more supple.

30. I can see and feel his/her hormones being in perfect balance for perfect performance and health.

31. I can see and feel his/her vitality.

32. I can see and feel his/her vibrant health.

33. I can see and feel his/her vascular system as smooth and clean as a newborn.

The value in exercising these images is that they reinforce your own work. They give you some practice in a dissociated way.

Related Affirmations:

a) He/she deserves to be healthy and fit.

b) I choose to model healthy people's behavior to get similar results.

c) I thank this person for modeling positive behavior

for me . . . that is for me!

It does no good at all to envy the person who is thin, healthy, and fit Instead, you can say, "That is for me. If he/she can do it, so can I." Interpret the fact that the person who makes good choices effortlessly is a sign of possibility . . . the possiblility that you can, too.

Stress Related Affirmations

Many people eat when they are under stress, positive or negative. Somewhere in their experience they have learned that eating reduces stress. The fact is, it does. But there are other ways to deal with stress. Instead of eating, the desire to eat during stressful periods of time *can* serve as a signal from the body that one needs to cope more effectively and in more appropriate ways . . . especially if eating behavior becomes out of control and if one is overweight. Then eating actually contributes to stress because, once one realizes what has happened, usually after the fact, the result is escalated distress and guilt.

a) When I feel the desire to eat, I ask myself, "Am I really hungry?"
b) If I am not hungry, I ask myself what I need and work to fulfill that need [exercise, rest, meditation, love].

c) If I am hungry, it is perfectly appropriate and necessary to nourish my body with nutrient-rich foods.

Nutritent-rich foods, when the goal is losing weight, are identified as foods which are low in fat (called low-caloric-density foods) and high in other nutrients such as vitamins, minerals, and amino acids. They tend to be high in water content. Examples include most fruits and vegetables.

d) A mistake is just a signal that I need to change my course of action and thinking. I learn from the mistake, let it go, and go on.

e) *Making* a mistake is not the same as *being* the mistake. I may fail, but I am not the failure.

f) Failure is nothing more than an opportunity to learn.

g) I accept life as an opportunity to grow and learn. Life is a challenge, not a burden.

Note the difference in the way you feel when you assign a situation or condition the label of "problem" versus the label of "challenge." A *problem* is heavy and burdensome. You become tired just thinking about it. A *challenge* creates a feeling of energy and excitement. You can hardly wait to get to it. Accepting life in total as a challenge can be a wonderfully freeing experience. Your entire orientation to life changes for the better. When you embrace this orientation, even problems have the possibility of becoming gifts, for they are the impetus for personal transformation.

h) Every problem I have is an opportunity for growing and learning.

Other

Remember, affirmations/images *you create* may be more powerful than ones given to you. Use your own creations in the same way you use these. You might also write down all the reasons why it is important for you to reach your goal on one card and all the consequences of NOT reaching your goal on another. This is called a "reinforcement menu" and can be used effectively when read anytime before you eat.

GOOD LUCK! However, luck has nothing to do with it.

PART III

EXPERIENCE

"When you wake up in the morning, Pooh,"
said Piglet at last, "what's the first thing
you say to yourself?"
"What's for breakfast?" said Pooh.
"What do you say, Piglet?"
"I say, I wonder what's going to happen
exciting today?" said Piglet.
Pooh nodded thoughtfully.
"It's the same thing," he said.

—A. A. Milne
Winnie-The-Pooh

.9.

Savoring

> *Lunch can be a hurried refueling, the equivalent of an auto racer's pit stop, or it can be an opportunity to savor the miracle that dirt, rain, seeds, and human imagination can work on our taste buds. We just have to be wise enough to know how to recognize the miracle, and not rush headlong past it in our search for "something."*
> —Harold Kushner

Suppose that your best and dearest friend is treating you and two of your other friends to a birthday celebration at the city's finest restaurant. Money is no object. This is a serious celebration occurring in elegant surroundings.

The wine steward pours a portion of the house's best wine into your glass. Everyone waits for your verdict as you lift the wine to the light and observe its color, whiff the bouquet, and finally, after you swirl it about in your mouth to share its flavor with each taste bud, you nod your approval. Everyone is delighted, especially the wine steward.

Later, weaving a bit on unsteady legs to visit the rest room, you're suddenly aware, "Oh my, the wine! . . . What was it? Oh yes, three bottles shared with four bodies. I got my share." Somewhere between the second and third hour of the festivities, the expensive chateau could have been replaced with $1.25 screw-top wine and you would not have known the difference.

What happened between the critic's first sip and the evening's euphoric end? The first sip was total engagement of the senses in the experience of the moment. Your awareness and attention were focused on the wine. You took in its essence with sight, smell, taste, and touch in an environment of acceptance and love. What a wonderful experience! Being totally involved in the moment, you weren't distracted by thoughts of work, responsibility, or worry. This is the experience of savoring.

Savoring is being conscious, AWAKE, to your participation in the present. Some moments after that first sip you became occupied with conversation and laughter interrupted with bits of delicious food. Once in a while, you fleetingly focused on the wine. Ah. Then back to the affairs at hand.

We have been gifted with an amazing ability to handle many things at once with little or no thought. The robot of habit can easily handle the simple tasks of bringing the fork or glass to the mouth, which frees us to concentrate on more important matters. The rub is that this gift possesses a negative aspect for those who have eating disorders or weight problems. Basic physiological mechanisms which normally control eating and weight are subverted with old, antiquated messages. False messages stored in the subconscious override messages of logic, real need, and those of the body.

Healthy people listen and respond appropriately to messages from the body. If it is hungry, they feed it. If it is full, they stop eating. Simple. Well, if it were just up to the body, it would be simple.

Some people, however, have lost their sensitivity to the body. They couldn't hear it even if it were screaming. There is a myriad of reasons for this deafness. A tale of Mulla Nasrudin, a Middle Eastern joke figure, illustrates the point.

One day the Mulla became exceedingly parched during his walk on a dry, hot, dusty road. There was no water to be had, so, seeing a vendor at the side of the road, he bought bunches of fruit, thinking this would alleviate his suffering. Having sold all his fruit, the vendor left. The Mulla sat down and began munching on the fruit. The fruit set his mouth ablaze. It burned all the way down to his belly, and he sweated profusely. But he kept eating.

A friend happened along and was confused by the Mulla's behavior.

"Mulla," he said, "why are you eating those hot chilies?"

The Mulla gasped, "I'm not eating chilies; I'm eating my money."

Most of us have mirrored the Mulla's behavior at one time or another. "I paid $15.00 for this meal; I'm gonna eat it!" The more times we ignore the body, the easier it gets. How else could a man possibly get to the point were he consumes more than a wheelbarrow full of food at a cost of 50,000 calories and $200 a day? (Sally Jessy Raphael, July 1988).

There are three ways the body tells us we are hungry. These are oral (mouth) hunger, low-blood-sugar hunger, and gastric (stomach) hunger. Savoring can help manage oral and blood-sugar hunger. Gastric hunger is affected more by increasing one's sensitivity to and respect for the body. Although gastric hunger is described in this chapter, it will be referred to more extensively later.

Oral Hunger

We experience oral hunger as a need to chew, to experience the sensations of texture and flavor. People who have had their jaws wired shut or people who have braces and are not allowed to eat certain kinds of food such as popcorn feel a great mouth hunger. Although they can still get completely nutritious foods during their temporary condition, they many times feel deprived. As one woman explained, she became "Jaws Personified" when the wires came off. "I ate everything in sight." In three short weeks, she regained the 40 pounds it had taken her four months to lose.

You have probably noticed that, during times when you had a cold and couldn't smell very well, food didn't taste quite the same. You may have been hungry, but since the food didn't *taste,* it wasn't worth the effort to eat. You ate less. Well, guess what? You're no different than a rat, at least in one way. In one experiment, rats were fed by means of a tube from a feeder directly to their stomachs. The food bypassed their mouths, thereby bypassing "oral" sensation. The rats could eat anytime they wished by pressing a bar to dispense the food into their stomachs. At no time were they deprived of food or enough food. These rats lost 25 per cent of their original weight and stayed at that weight as long as they were only allowed to eat in this manner. There was no way for them to satisfy mouth hunger; therefore, signals to feed were picked up by the other two sensory modes, gastric and blood sugar.

Taste is instrumental in what we eat and how much

we eat. Given a choice, both humans and animals eat more if food is sweetened. One man commented, "I wish my stomach were bigger so I could eat more."

Sometimes we crave a flavor or texture of a specific food. If the food is *verboten* and we try to satisfy our mouth hunger by eating other foods, we may end up with the "grazing effect." We eat 10,000 calories trying to satisfy a hunger that would have only cost us 250 calories if we would only "buy direct." Cravings for specific foods are learned responses. For example, an Asian who has never set foot outside of Cambodia wouldn't crave a Dairy Queen Peanut-butter Parfait. However, roast monkey might very well trigger salivation for the Asian, while it will probably elicit the gag reflex in Americans. Types of food cravings, such as salty or sweet, rather than specific foods, may have some biological basis.

Craving for food in general may indicate psychological rather than physiological hunger. Of course, to feed a psychological need such as the need for comfort or control with food doesn't work. Recurrent binging is usually a sign of psychological hunger. Savoring doesn't occur during binging because there is a sense of urgency in filling a need. One can't slow down, can't taste. Its function is to stop pain rather than to enhance enjoyment. This will be addressed later in detail.

Savoring helps with weight and eating control because, to savor, you must eat more slowly. One satisfies mouth hunger with less food and, as you will see, this interacts nicely with alleviating low blood sugar. Savoring also helps at the level of mouth hunger. It helps signal when to stop. You cannot savor something you dislike for long. I had a client who, when she dieted, consumed large quantities of Concord grapes as a replacement for "bad" food. She reasoned quite rightly that grapes were a better choice than candy. After practicing savoring for a week, she reported, "You know all those grapes? I hate grapes!" Savoring breaks the habit robot by gently nudging you into consciousness. You wake up!

Gastric Hunger

Gastric hunger is caused by stomach contractions. We literally feel and interpret the contractions as hunger. The contractions are unpleasant and act as a signal for the body to eat. People vary in their perceptions of and intensity of stomach contractions. Infants cry when they are hungry, and they certainly have a right to. Their stomach contractions are two to three times as intense as those of adults. They hurt. In contrast, nicotine inhibits contractions so that smokers do not experience the same intensity of contractions that nonsmokers do. This may be one reason smokers tend to gain weight when they give up tobacco.

Obese people just don't seem to know when contractions happen and when they don't. This is one way they exhibit lack of sensitivity to the body. They confuse external cues with real physiological cues for hunger.

When normal-weight and obese volunteers were asked if they were hungry, the normal-weight individuals reported hunger when in fact their stomachs were actually contracting. Obese individuals, however, seemed to report hunger when they saw that it was time to eat, smelled food, or food was clearly visible. The presence or absence of contractions did not predict obese volunteers' perception of hunger.

One of my clients explained that she only ate one meal a day, after work, about 8:00 p.m. As a person who experiences hunger about every two hours, I found it difficult to imagine making it through the day without some form of nourishment.

"My goodness, aren't you famished?" I exclaimed.

"No," she replied demurely.

"Don't you get hungry? I'd be starving," I said. "How do you manage?"

"I just don't get hungry."

Since she expressed interest, I tried to explain the sensations of hunger. That's like trying to explain how orgasm feels to someone who is anorgasmic. After practicing with exercises which are designed to heighten awareness of bodily sensations, she came in one evening and said excitedly, "I think I felt it. You know, hunger." But, she wasn't exactly sure. Again, there are many reasons for extinguishing bodily sensitivity.

People who have been abused as children learn from a very early age to dissociate from their bodies. Its a way to maintain sanity and survive.

Low-Blood-Sugar Hunger

Low-blood-sugar hunger is felt to the "depth of the bones." One gets shaky, or faint and just generally doesn't feel too good. People who are blood-sugar hungry are not very pleasant people to be around. They are crabby and sometimes downright unreasonable. This is because the only kind of food that the central nervous system can eat is blood glucose or blood sugar. Severe cases of low blood sugar, hypoglycemia, can lead to coma and even death.

A friend of mine who was training for a bodybuilding competition epitomized the hypoglycemic world view. He was only eating 500 to 700 calories a day, training 3 to 4 hours a day, sleeping two hours a night (one burns more calories awake than asleep), and consuming rather large doses of caffeine. Sitting down glumly at the desk over a cup of coffee one night, he shook his head and murmured, "Well, I'm just generally pissed off."

Of course he was! Actually, it was his central nervous system that should have been pissed off for being treated so shabbily. Something as important as the nervous system deserves to be fed once in a while.

The degree of concentration of sugar circulating in the blood registers in the brain in a specialized group of cells called the hypothalamus. The hypothalamus monitors many body functions, such as thirst, satiety (the sense of being satisfied), hunger, heart rate, etc. If blood sugar is low, the healthy hypothalamus signals the body to start eating. It also works to signal other body processes to release energy reserves to reestablish normal ranges of sugar. The feeding of the central nervous system is a top priority. If it starves, the body stops.

It takes approximately 20 minutes from the time you start eating for food to effectively enter the blood stream and register in the hypothalamus. When you savor, you eat slowly enough to allow the food to register with the master controller of satiety and hunger. You start to feel better as hunger is appeased and, at the same time, satisfy mouth hunger.

There are techniques in behavior modification which work on the same principle. Eat without reading or watching television. Chew your food 32 times and put eating utensils down between bites. To do all this, you must slow down, which, in effect, allows enough time for the hypothalamus to get the signal. I find these techniques too contrived, unnatural, and mechanistic to be effective over the long haul. Eating becomes a tedious chore rather than a pleasant experience. The only thing more tedious is counting calories. Behavior modification techniques do little to enhance enjoyment because you concentrate on counting, and so on rather than flavor and texture. Energy is wasted on unimportant, frivolous matters. Savoring accomplishes the same goal with a sense of pleasure rather than drudgery. I cannot imagine anyone spending an entire lifetime counting masticatory compressions.

Savoring is my favorite technique because it is profoundly simple, yet its effects on one's quality of life are astronomical. The "doing" of savoring is easy, although the "remembering" to do is not. I refer to savoring as a technique but it is much more. It is part of the art of living.

It is a way to "feel the rapture of being alive." As Joseph Campbell states in *The Power of Myth:*

> People say that what we're all seeking is a meaning for life. I don't think that's what we're really seeking. I think that what we're seeking is an experience of being alive, so that our life experiences on the purely physical plane will have resonances within our own innermost being and reality, so that we actually feel the rapture of being alive.

We will apply savoring as a "technique" to help us achieve weight and eating goals. However, realize at the outset that it is much more . . . the technique is a lesson in how to live life. It would be a tragic loss to let it end as a mere instructional activity.

Harold Kushner, in his wonderful book *When All You've Ever Wanted Isn't Enough,* echoes the sentiments of Campbell when he addresses one of the major questions of life, "What is life about?"

> It is not about writing great books, amassing great wealth, achieving great power. It is about loving and being loved. It is about enjoying your food and sitting

in the sun rather than rushing through lunch and hurrying back to the office. It is about savoring the beauty of moments that don't last, the sunsets, the leaves turning color, the rare moments of true human communication. It is about savoring them rather than missing out on them because we are so busy and they will not hold still until we get around to them . . . When we come to that stage in our lives when we are less able to accomplish but more able to enjoy, we will have attained . . . wisdom. . . .

So weight control or eating problems may have brought you to a new dimension in the art of living. Let's get on with it.

Savoring Techniques

Savoring is one of the best techniques available for breaking the destructive habits of a lifetime. It is one of the first steps in developing an awareness of what you are doing which will enable you to act upon what you truly want and need. Awareness is absolutely essential to making accurate, appropriate choices. It is surprisingly simple to do as long as you remind yourself to do it. Many of the affirmations and imagery exercises are presented for the purpose of reminding ourselves what we want so we will not fall back into actions based on false assumptions and messages of the past. Although the following activities focus on food and drink, remember to practice on virtually everything, such as precious moments with loved ones, rainbows, etc.

NOTE: Read through all the directions first. Then, set up the appropriate conditions and begin.

EXERCISE ONE

Savoring a Treat. Select a food which is your all time favorite decadent, abusive, "shouldn't ever eat this kind of junk" kind of treat. Perhaps it is a hot fudge sundae, a banana split, or pecan pie a la mode. Do not settle for something else because it happens to be in the house and/or is *almost* as good as your favorite. Make the effort. Get the best. Pick only one, please. Set up an environment which is ideal for savoring for the first time. Choose a place which is private. There should be no distractions such as television, newspapers, etc. Make sure you have plenty of time and will not be interrupted. It is best to do this by yourself. Your only focus should be on the food.

Before you begin to indulge, close your eyes and imagine the treat before you. In your mind's eye, imagine its texture, color, temperature, shape, and flavor. Upon opening your eyes, look at the food, smell it, take in its color and shape, etc. Linger over it. Take your time. Recognize that this food will be transformed by your body into energy, a miraculous occurrence even though this food is not a "good" choice.

Now take a bite slowly and experience its essence. Just as in the example with the expensive chateau wine where you were *experiencing* all fine wines in one representative sip, this treat represents all fine treats of its kind. As you eat, try to remain as focused on each bite as you were on the first. Tune in to how you feel at the moment. Notice if your feelings change, or your perceptions change as you eat. For example, you might find that your enjoyment of the

Continued →

Exercise One—cont'd.

sweetness changes with time; it may taste better or worse than you anticipated. Eat the entire treat.

Now write a brief summary in your journal on the experience. Then read your summary. Writing is much more beneficial than merely thinking through the exercise. Writing is a wonderful self-discovery tool which also provides you with a record of your progress. As Gertrude Stein said, creation takes place between the pen and the paper.

You might try answering the following questions, which are meant to stimulate some thought and awareness rather than create anxiety. It is not a quiz.

1. Did the treat taste better or worse than other times?

2. If so, how would you account for the difference?

3. What were your emotional reactions to the exercise? Did you think it was fun, exciting, silly?

4. What kinds of associations do you have with this particular food, if any? For example, although I haven't had chocolate pie for years, I think of the great pie my Grandma Ruby used to make every time I see chocolate pie. Did your mom make or buy this for you as a kid? Was it a reward for being "good," etc.? Is it associated with a holiday such as Valentine's Day? Another way to discover associations is through mind-mapping.

EXERCISE TWO

Savoring Good Food. It is probably best to do Exercise Two on a different day than Exercise One. Follow exactly the same instructions, only this time select a favorite "good" food, something you really like which is a nutritionally sound choice. Perhaps it is a fresh spinach salad, or a cold, crisp apple. Be certain to make a journal entry answering the same questions as in Exercise One. Add questions 5 and 6:

5. What were the primary differences you felt between the junk treat and the "good" treat?

6. If you were hungry and had the choice right now, which food would you want? Let the "child" in you answer. Base your answer solely on the savoring experience rather than any old messages or judgments you might hear reverberating in the background.

EXERCISE THREE

Savoring Everything. This is the ongoing "for the rest of your life" exercise. Savor everything, especially food and drink.

Practice savoring little things in all kinds of situations and circumstance. Savor the ground beneath your feet, the birds' song, the sun and the rain, the shape of a leaf, the touch of a friend, the trust in your child's eyes, and the challenge and liveliness savoring brings to the ordinarily mundane.

Choose to be awake to life. If you are awake, you naturally make better decisions as well as decisions which affirm life. And with eating, savoring appeases the hunger monster.

Savoring is easy when that is all you have to do as in Exercise One and Two. However, life has a way of interfering with the best of intentions.

Old habits and the associations they elicit are deeply ingrained in neurological pathways. The fact that these habits recur despite your heroic efforts is a function of a very real physiologic conditioning rather than a lack of will power on your part. It takes a while for grass to grow again on a well-worn path, to extinguish old ways, and to forge another path. It is not the fault of the grass that it does not grow faster. Be patient but persistent. Be kind and forgiving with yourself, but get tough at the same time. Flex your spiritual muscles to gain the strength and courage to continue. Whatever you do, continue. Don't roll over and play dead. Playing dead is a great way to become dead.

Continued →

> **Exercise Three—cont'd.**
>
> Savoring is an art that takes a great deal of practice, and I am not sure if it is ever totally natural; that is, I think we must all remind ourselves to notice our surroundings and experience. The payoffs seem to be well worth the investment.

If we savored more we would communicate more deeply, relate more fully, compete less regularly, and celebrate more authentically. . . . We would be more in touch with our moral outrage because our love of life would increase so dramatically that we would become less and less tolerant of death forces.

—Matthew Fox, *Original Blessing,* p. 52.

We cannot binge and savor simultaneously because binging is an escape, a negation of life, while savoring is an affirmation of life. There is no true pleasure in overindulgence. Overindulgence with anything dulls the senses instead of sharpening the senses. Overindulgence kills pleasure.

The source of all authentic pleasure is God.

—Matthew Fox

Suggested Reading:

Kushner, Harold. *When All You Ever Wanted Isn't Enough.* New York: Pocket Books, 1986.

·10·

Listening to the Body

All the work we have done up to this point, with the exception of savoring, has dealt with the mind controlling and directing the body. The mind is the sculptor, the body the clay.

There is a danger in taking this analogy too far, because the body is not clay. It is a living, dynamic energy system which continually gives off signals which the mind can interpret and act on if it is aware and conscious. Without awareness, the mind may be in control but it is functioning through one-way communication which is limiting and often misleading. Effective communication is only possible through two-way communication. This holds true as much for work with the body as work with people. The objective is not to subdue and conquer the body, but to work in cooperation with it.

Cooperation is impossible without feedback. We must learn to listen and respond. Merely through the act of listening, we begin to transform an adversarial relationship into a cooperative relationship. Listening is one of the most profound demonstrations of respect we can choose to exercise. Listening enables you to respond appropriately. The body becomes a friend instead of an enemy. It is much easier to fulfill potential with the body as an ally.

Ira Proff, a depth psychologist, developed a method of journaling called the Intensive Journal. One of the techniques included in this chapter, "Communicating with the Body," is modified from one of Progoff's techniques called dialoguing. In "dialoguing with the body," a type of imaginary conversation with the body, Progoff described the following:

> One college student . . . turned his dialogue script into a poetic exaltation of the grandeurs of the human mind. He waxed poetic about the marvels of philosophy and science which the human mind has achieved. In contrast, he told his body that it plays only an insignificant role in his life. Thereupon the body responded in the dialogue script and said, "That's all very well. Your mind is high and mighty. But try going to the toilet without me!"
>
> —Progoff, 1975, p. 202

Obviously the body has something to tell us from the everyday kind to necessities of going to the toilet to resting. Other messages may be much more subtle but no less important in the long run. The subtle messages are easily overshadowed by the very nature of daily living.

To survive, we must be outwardly directed. We have to go to work, take the kids to school, clean the house, buy the groceries, etc. But the subtle messages are important to survival as well. Blocking messages, for whatever reason, is a kind of deafness that puts us at risk. We fail to receive vital information on the status of the body. For example, stress, which is a body response, can make us sick. Despite the presence of physical signs and symptoms, the majority of us are not aware of warnings. If we listen, we can then act to alleviate and manage the stress effectively.

If the mind is held in an exalted position, the body may be in trouble for another reason. The mind may be mistaken. The distorted perceptions of anorexic nervous individuals which lead to self-starvation are an extreme example. The mind is killing the body. The opposite extreme is overeating and binging. The body certainly tells you when it is starving or when it is too full. We ignore or subdue signals out of faulty perception, dislike, hatred, lack of respect, and anger. This most valuable possession, the body, does pretty well taking care of itself despite being subjected to recurrent and chronic abuse. It could use some help.

The purpose of this chapter is to learn to listen to the messages the body continually sends us so that we are better able to nurture it. Through the experiential exercises, we can begin to hear the messages. Further, we begin to appreciate the marvel that is the body. With appreciation comes value. We take care of that which we cherish.

I used to walk through the fairgrounds near my house frequently and had many opportunities to watch horse and dog shows. I was struck by the contrast between owners/trainers and their animals. No expense was spared on these much-loved, beautiful, well-conditioned animals that proudly moved around the arena. They were obviously fed the best diets, exercised, and groomed. However, many of the handlers reflected the exact opposite. Many huffed and puffed, occasionally stumbling, as they moved the animals through their paces in the arena. Overweight and smoking, these handlers literally detracted from the beauty in motion. What if they treated themselves with the same respect and care given a champion? What if they cherished and valued their bodies/themselves as much as they do these wonderful animals?

Appreciation of the body is an emotional experience that cannot occur if it is taken for granted. To be whole and healthy, all aspects of the personality must be integrated. Alienation from the body is fragmentation which totally excludes appreciation. The body is just something to cover up with clothes. One can even get away with totally ignoring it until it breaks down. Then it is subject to verbal and emotional abuse for having the nerve to do so. Well, that is the only way to get the attention it needs.

EXERCISE ONE

List Reasons for Eating. Are you alienated from your body? In your journal, write down as many reasons as you can think of that cause you to eat or continue eating. Do not continue reading until you have done the exercise.

Now, how many reasons for eating do you have, *excluding* hunger? Did you include hunger? If hunger is a physiological experience governed by the energy requirements of the body, why are there so many other reasons for eating besides hunger? What are your ideas on this subject?

Joyce Slochower stated, "When an adult undergoes intense emotional distress, he or she may turn to food in an attempt to recapture the security and comfort experienced in infancy" (1983, p. 13). She cited a study which reviewed the unconscious meanings of overeating and obesity (Kaplan & Kaplan, 1957). The following 27 meanings of overeating have been proposed by different theorists. Do you identify with any of these?

1. diminishing anxiety
2. achieving pleasure
3. relieving frustration and deprivation
4. achieving social success and acceptance
5. expressing hostility
   (conscious and unconscious)
6. diminishing feeling of insecurity
7. self-indulgence
8. rewarding oneself
9. expressing defiance

Continued →

Exercise One—cont'd.

10. submitting; e.g., to parental authority
11. self-punishment in response to guilt
12. diminishing guilt
13. exhibitionism
14. attaining attention and care
15. justifying failure in life
16. testing love
17. distorting reality
18. courteracting a feeling of being unloved
19. identifying with a fat parent
20. sedating oneself
21. avoiding competition in life
22. avoiding changing the status quo
23. proving one's inferiority
24. avoiding maturity
25. diminishing fear of starvation
26. consciously fulfilling the wish to become fat
27. handling anxiety from infantile oral frustration

You have probably added others similar to the ones my clients and students have come up with: because it's (the food) there; boredom; it is time to eat; I won't get to eat 'til later; because everyone else is eating; to show off; anxiety; nervousness; depression; to feel better; because I'm tired; etc.

Ideally, the primary choice, at least at the level of the body, is to eat because of hunger and to stop when full. It is okay to eat because it tastes good, it is dinner time, and so on as long as hunger accompanies those other reasons. Obviously, if one really lis-

Continued →

Exercise One—cont'd.

tened and responded to the signals of the body, weight control would be much easier. But again, the signal must be heard over these other needs. Languaging and imagery techniques help one identify and deal with psychic needs. Overeating and eating disorders are warnings that our needs are not being met in appropriate ways. Overeating is not just a problem. It is a message, and within the message lies the opportunity to learn.

How do we improve our listening skills so that we can learn to appreciate and nurture the vehicle of the soul and psyche? There are several ways.

EXERCISE TWO

Tuning into the Body. The world is experienced through the senses. There is no other way to know the world. The body is the purveyor of sight, sound, touch, taste, and smell. Sensation is of the body. Sensation is a physical event. Interpretation of the sensation is a function of the mind. Each individual has a different sensory history which is assigned meaning based upon unique styles, learning, and values. One way to tune into the body is to experience sensation without assigning meaning . . . just experience it. An example of this would be to feel pain without the usual self-talk: "Boy, this hurts! What if it doesn't go away? I need to call in and cancel that appointment."

I tried a suggestion a fellow student shared with me in graduate school. "When you're running and you get a pain in your side, 'crawl' into the pain and keep going." The pain wasn't nearly so "bad" and it actually disappeared. Pain became just another physical experience rather than something that was awful. Pain represented only one of the incredible variety of sensations that make life interesting. What if one did the same type of thing with hunger?

This exercise will enhance the experiential instead of the interpretational aspect of sensation. Give yourself at least 30 minutes to write a sensory history. Write down very brief descriptors of the physical experiences of your life. Chronological order is not important. Write down anything that comes to mind from your earliest childhood or infant memories

Continued →

Exercise Two—cont'd.

to the present time. There is no need to explain the entries in detail. The word or phrase will be enough for you to know the context or story behind it, the meaning. Avoid judging and labeling the entries as good or bad, although you can record the emotion you felt at the time it happened. Think of things you felt, saw, smelled, heard, tasted. You will notice that one entry will stimulate another similar one because of association, as you experienced with mind-mapping. A short example is offered below:

The baby bed is white, the light bulb bright.
The bass of the stereo.
Being knocked out.
Nausea, throwing up.
Food poisoning.
Shock of cold water in the pool.
Holding a baby—soft, smooth skin.
Being touched by a lover; touching a lover.
A caffeine buzz.
Jumping off a cliff . . . scared!
Playing hide-and-seek at night . . . feeling my heart beat, sure the guy that was "it" could hear it.
Spider bites.
Scarlet fever, sore throat.
The cool breeze over bare skin on a summer night.
Weakness . . . energy draining from my hands. Will I die?
Running away from a horse.
Adrenaline rush.

Continued →

Exercise Two—cont'd.

Full moon on the lake—magnificent beauty in the midst of emotional pain.

Clean sheets, line dried.

Feeling the life slip away from a pet, watching him die, not being able to help.

Car wreck . . . slow motion.

And so on.

It becomes evident that this could go on and on and on. Your whole life is a series of physical sensations. If you do this several times over a week, you will find yourself experiencing sensation without judgment. Also, you can get in touch with your history. This can be painful and difficult in the beginning.

I explained this exercise to a client and then left her alone in the office for 20 minutes to allow her some privacy. She only had five entries in 20 minutes. One of the entries was "sick." In an effort to help her understand the instructions, I asked her how it felt to be "sick." She said, "You know, sick." Different illnesses have different signs and symptoms such as sore throat, cramps, nausea, chills, weakness, fatigue, burning, numbness, etc. She could not identify one! I prodded her with questions but promptly backed off when she started getting angry out of frustration. Much to my surprise, she told me a week later that she had been working on this exercise. While doing the exercise, she had remembered that she was abused as a child. This, of course, meant remembering and re-experiencing the pain. Dissociating from

Continued →

Exercise Two—cont'd.

her body was a means of survival as a child. However, as an adult, it no longer served a function. This was a very difficult process for her, but she said it was well worth it.

Why is it worth it? If the bad is blocked out, so is the good. Alienation is insensitive. Sensory messages bounce off the injured psyche. It is like flying blind.

EXERCISE THREE

The Stress Wheel. Draw a circle and divide it into ten equal increments. Number the increments from one to ten. One represents what it was like to be the most relaxed you have ever been. Ten represents the most distress you have ever felt. Right now, what number are you? How do you know the number you marked is accurate? That is, how do you determine your stress level? Is stress mental or physical or both?

Technically, stress is the bodily response to a stimulus. Stress can be measured with physiological instruments because physical blood pressure, heart rate, circulatory rate, and muscle tension all increase. There are hormonal changes that occur as well. If the stimulus is interpreted as physically or psychologically threatening, it is distress. It is unpleasant. If the stimulus is interpreted as "good," similar physiological changes occur, but it is perceived as pleasant. This is "good" stress, or *eustress*. Both distress and eustress require that one adapt to change. Stress will *always* manifest itself through the body in one way or another. It is the process of interpretation that makes stress a mental experience as well.

Briefly describe a recent distressful experience.

How did you feel physically? Be as specific as possible. For example, instead of "I was nervous," it would be "My hands shook." Or, "My stomach was upset . . . I could not eat." How did you feel mentally? Confused, angry, frustrated, saddened? How did you handle or cope with the situation? This may give you

Continued →

Exercise Three—cont'd.

a clearer idea of what a "ten" represents.

Keeping a stress-wheel diary for a couple of weeks will assist you in tuning into the body. You may discover patterns of stress and further notice eating behavior following these patterns. Not only do you listen to the body better, but awareness of patterns will enable you to break those patterns.

It would be a disservice to address weight-control solutions without addressing the problem of stress. Referring back to the list of 27 reasons for eating and the list you generated, notice that most are directly or indirectly related to stress. Suppose the first time a person binges is to assuage guilt (although any distressful emotion can serve as an example). Eating changes mood and one's internal emotional state. It is comforting or sedating. Although initially the eating was done in response to distress, it can quickly generalize to eustress. The number of triggers for binging increases so that a person eats when sad or happy, anxious or eager, depressed or elated. The only way for a person in this state to be successful is to learn to effectively manage stress.

This is not a stress-management book, but imagery, languaging, and relaxation inductions are all forms of stress management. See the suggested reading list at the end of this chapter for resources in this area.

Even sitting quietly by yourself, for yourself, is a stress-management tool. Predictable patterns of vulnerability revealed in the stress-wheel journal will

Continued →

Exercise Three—cont'd.

give you clues as to the best times to use languaging and imagery.

For example, Bob works the early shift and gets home before his wife and children. As a supervisor of 28 people in his work unit, he experiences a lot of pressure at work. He has developed a habit of eating snacks from 2:30 until 4 as he reads the newspaper and watches television.

Although his stress wheel reveals that his stress levels are higher during work than at home following work, stress is cumulative, and he is carrying the stress home with him. Eating, reading, and watching television all serve to relieve the stress.

The result of his coping style is negative because he has gained weight due to excessive caloric intake and lack of exercise. Because of the stress, he may not "want" to exercise. He is tired after work. Upon examination however, the fatigue is mental.

Exercise is refreshing, and it diverts his attention away from food and eating. If he finds it difficult to overcome his inertia, a brief relaxation technique accompanied with affirmations and goal imagery may revitalize him enough to get moving. The stress wheel identified his vulnerable time in terms of stress instead of eating. The solution is not merely to quit eating. The solution is to manage stress, which will in turn automatically take care of the eating problem.

When you identify an eating pattern, look beyond the pattern to the events and feelings that lead to acting out the pattern. As discussed previously, feelings

Continued →

Exercise Three—cont'd.

toward events can be altered by exploring alternative meanings to the events. Is the event really awful or is it awful from one perspective? What are other frames of references?

Many of the students in my stress-management classes have told me that they never realized they were under stress until they did the stress-wheel diaries. The stress wheel is another way to increase awareness quickly and easily.

EXERCISE FOUR

Communicating with the Body. What would happen if the "The Body" could sit across from you and carry on a conversation with you as a friend or acquaintance? What would it say or ask? Would it have anything to tell you? Might it warn you that you have high blood pressure, a gene that will threaten you mental capacities when you age, fat accumulating around your heart? Would it thank you for the workout? What would you tell it? That you are angry it got the flu, that it can't stay up all night and function the next day? Would the conversation be casual, friendly, humorous? Or, would there be silence?

The purpose of this exercise is much like the others. However, it entails a verbal component. It is language, imagery, and experience. Perhaps this combination is why it is so powerful when it works.

After a relaxation induction of your choosing, imagine sitting across from your body, the physical aspect of yourself. You may begin by asking a question, saying hello, or anything that elicits a dialogue. How would you begin a conversation with another person? It depends on the person and the situation, doesn't it? If the situation is informal and the person is a friend, the conversation is easy. The conversation has a life of its own. You do not have to think ahead of time what you are going to say and how the other person might respond. This exercise is much the same. When you are very relaxed and set up the situation, the conversation "just happens." There is a natural beginning, middle and end. It is not contrived

Continued →

Exercise Four—cont'd.

or forced.

Write the conversation down as it happens in the form of a script. For example:

Me: Hi, Bod. How you doing? You are not looking too well these days . . . a little tired.

Body: Well, yes. I need more than four hours sleep a night. You know I will get sick if this keeps up.

Me: I don't know what to do about that, though. I have to get this project done . . . the publisher wants this book by the 15th.

And so on . . .

In the beginning, the writing of the script may detract from the conversation. With a little practice, it will be easy to do both.

Here are the steps for the exercise:

1. Sit in a comfortable position with a pad and pencil or with a word processor.

2. Read through your entries for Exercise Two, "Tuning into the Body."

3. Close your eyes and do a relaxation exercise.

4. Imagine yourself sitting across from your body.

5. Take your time and surrender to the exercise. Some conversations are easy and flow naturally. Some start and stop, start and stop. Sometimes nothing happens. During moments of silence, close your eyes, relax, and wait. If nothing seems to happen, that is okay. Try it again at another time. At least you are relaxing and therefore allowing stress to dissolve

Continued →

Exercise Four—cont'd.

from your body.

    6. Open your eyes just enough to write out the dialogue as it happens.

    7. Allow the conversation to end naturally.

    8. Relax a moment or two. Open your eyes and stretch.

    9. Read your script. What did you learn? Any surprises? Did it affirm or remind you of what you already know?

    One of my students, a 22-year-old woman, discovered one of the barriers she had thwarting weight loss through this exercise. When she was 13, her father made an inappropriate sexual advance toward her, fondling her breasts. It frightened her. Her "body" told her that it wanted the extra weight to protect her from sexual assault. This was the first time she realized the connection. The right hemisphere of the brain finally had the opportunity to fit the pieces of the puzzle together. The problem of weight control was seen in a different context, which now allows for a different, more effective solution.

EXERCISE FIVE

The Hunger Meter. This exercise was developed by Colin Rose *(The Mind & Body Diet,* 1989). It helps one to focus awareness on body needs at the time one eats.

> Think of your stomach as a fuel tank—and think of an imaginary fuel gauge on it. A gauge that uses a 0-10 scale. 0 is absolutely empty. You're really hungry and ready to eat. 1 would be ready to eat, 2 would be at the level of 'fancying something' but not desperate, and so on. The critical point on the fuel gauge is 5. A 5 would be that lightly satisfied, comfortable feeling where you know you've had just enough. You feel really good when you get up from eating and you've got the energy to keep going.
>
> If you start eating when you're a 1 and you stop eating at 5, you'll never ever put weight on again.   —(pp. 49-50)

Rose suggests that you place your fist on your stomach before you eat and visualize the gauge. The clenched fist is about the size of an empty stomach. This is an extremely simple exercise. It functions to immediately bring your awareness to what your body needs are at the time you are ready to act out the triggers of hunger or appetite.

The exercises in this chapter range from the simple, quick ones such as the Hunger-Meter to the complex. All of them function to facilitate two-way communication between the mind and body. Each is unique, however, so it is a good idea to give them all a try. Although these techniques appear to limit eating, they may do the opposite. One should eat when hungry. If one respects, loves, and appreciates the body, self-starvation is unacceptable.

Suggested Reading:

Davis, M., Eshelman, E. R., and McKay, M. *The Relaxation & Stress Reduction Workbook.* Oakland, CA: New Harbinger Publications, 1988.

Rose, Colin. *The Mind & Body Diet.* 50 Aylesbury Road, Aston Clinton, Bucks, Great Britain: Accelerated Learning Systems Limited, 1989.

Rose, Colin. *Fat Busters Mind & Body Slimming Manual* (and audiocassette). 50 Aylesbury Road, Aston Clinton, Bucks, Great Britain: Accelerated Learning Systems Limited, 1991.

Progoff, Ira. *At A Intensive Journal Workshop.* New York: Dialogue House Library, 1975.

·11·

Conclusion

At this point, if you have worked and played with the activities in each chapter, you should have gained a sense of self-confidence along with increased ease in carrying out the action needed for your success. You have set yourself outside of the norm by becoming more independent, optimistic, and in control.

There will be times when you will feel that it is certainly more comfortable to reside within the norm. However, with time and practice, it becomes natural to the point where you will consider reverting back to the old, familiar lifestyle as totally unacceptable, without possibility. When one exchanges anything for something of higher value, it is not a sacrifice. When you exchanged a negative lifestyle and mind-set for one that is more life-affirming, you negotiated a good deal. The changes in your attitude, perception, and self-esteem function to diminish or eliminate the struggle that was formerly a daily companion. Environmental conditions and other people's opinions do not matter as much.

However, as human beings, we never outgrow our need for a sense of belonging, acceptance and recognition. Bernie Siegel, the physician who has worked extensively with cancer patients, suggested in a presentation that everyone, even healthy people, could benefit from a support group. Unfortunately, most support groups are established to deal with problems. There is really not an appropriate alternative for healthy individuals. But there is a need.

I suggest that you form your own Master Mind Group. The Master Mind concept was originally described as a group of people who come together with a common purpose or goal. I conceive of the group a bit differently in that it functions to support anyone in fulfilling potential, whatever that potential happens to be. The group is an enclave of positivity which charges one with the energy needed to confront and deal with a basically negative culture for a week or so at a time. I encourage you to form a Master Mind Group to help reinforce and remind you of what you have learned. The following are guidelines to follow for establishing such a group:

1. The group is comprised of six to eight people who tend to be positive most of the time or people who at the very least *want* to be positive. They accept responsibility for their actions and have an appreciation for the power of choice. You hand-pick your members. Once formed, other members can invite friends to join as long as the group does not get so large as to limit effective interaction.

2. Usually, the group needs some direction to be effective. You may alternate "leaders" or choose someone who functions as a good leader. You may choose a

book, topic, or speaker to provide structure. But the main function of the group is to provide a supportive, trusting atmosphere in which to share goals, accomplishments, or problems.

3. Developing trust is absolutely essential for this group to work. Therefore, each member is treated with respect, and all reference to individuals and happenings are confidential unless agreed upon by each person prior to the close of the meeting. Never assume that he/she won't mind if you tell so-and-so.

4. Keep the meetings positive. Each member is responsible for making every other member accountable for this. This does not mean that problems are not shared. They should be, because others can serve as sounding boards and offer suggestions for possible solutions. "Bitch and Moan" and/or gossip sessions are strictly off limits. One hears enough of this kind of talk during the normal course of the week. You don't need a Master Mind Group for that.

5. Meet regularly. If possible, once per week is best. Continuity, energy, and rapport are difficult to develop and maintain with monthly meetings, but they are better than nothing.

6. Focus on what you want rather than what you don't want.

7. Be flexible. You create the group. You can, therefore, create the format and agendas.

In closing, I wish you well and offer congratulations. The challenging task of tackling a weight or body- composition-control problem is an opportunity in disguise. Effective problem-solving requires growth of the *self*. In the words of Marsha Sinetar, "The advancement of wholeness is the real occupation of human existence." Therefore, you have done much more than solve a weight problem.

8. Share your success! I would like to learn of your experiences and successes (your problems and concerns, too). Your experiences can serve to help me refine techniques and to continually add to my knowledge. It is people just like you who helped me learn as much as I have about imagery and the imagery experience for which I am so grateful.

Writing and sharing your experience serves an important function for you, also. It validates your success and the process of your internal experience. Unfortunately, sharing certain kinds of experiences in our culture is discouraged in many ways. We all need to learn that internal experience is very real to the person who is experiencing it.

If you wish to share, please write to me in care of the publisher:

Dr. Constance Kirk, c/o Llewellyn Publications, Inc., P.O. Box 64383, St. Paul, MN 55164-0383

Good luck, stay conscious, and savor!

Appendix A

Interpreting and Transforming Negative Language

A. *"I am going to try to lose ten pounds by Christmas."*
The key word here is *try*. One will choose to lose 10 pounds or one will choose *not* to lose 10 pounds. It is a decision to do or not to do and there is no *try* to it.

If you are holding a pencil and I ask you to try to throw me the pencil, you must decide whether to throw the pencil or not. You could only legitimately *try* to throw the pencil if it were either a very heavy pencil or if it were tied to the table. Then you would not know if you could do it. Can I really lose 10 pounds? Answered honestly, I know I can lose 10 pounds if I stay on a proper diet/exercise routine. To use the term *try* under these circumstances is evidence of lack of commitment or lack of faith in oneself, or it may provide an escape route for not taking the responsibility for following through on a goal. This sounds rather harsh, but it is honest.

One might argue that, "I tried it before (thousands of times) and I couldn't do it." This "failure" sets one up with negative expectation and, although I want to believe I can, I expect that I can't. This turns out to be a powerful self-fulfilling prophecy. Using "try" is natural when I have failed so many times before, but it sets me up for another failure. My own language is a barrier to achievement. We can effectively counter the barrier with appropriate affirmations. We also change the meaning of appropriate affirmations. We also change the meaning of failure. Failure just means I haven't figured out what works yet. Instead of trying harder doing the same thing, I will try a different solution.

Losing 10 pounds by Christmas is another question. The time restraint may change the meaning entirely. I may have, in fact, committed to losing weight, knowing full well that it is possible and that I have faith in myself, but I may not know that I can do it by Christmas. Just make certain that, whenever the term *try* is used, it is not a form of self-deception.

Appropriate language: "I will be _____ pounds by Christmas."

B. *"Just my luck. They'll probably be out of my size by the time we get there."*

This is clearly an example of negative expectation. Negative thoughts yield negative results. As pointed out in the section on imagery, an extremely important attribute of successful imagery is positive expectation. When you discover yourself thinking or voicing negative expectation, you need to immediately change the negative to a positive. This immediate change in expectation increases awareness and helps to establish a new habit pattern. It will also help you pull out of the tendency toward self-pity.

Appropriate language: "I hope they have my size."

C. *"You just have to try the cherry pie! It's delicious."*

Is the statement true? What would happen if I did not try it? Nothing, except I am closer to my weight or body-composition goal by choosing to *not* do something. It is a false statement and a ridiculous one as well.

Appropriate language: "I think the pie is delicious.

Would you like a piece?"

D. *"I'll just die if I can't make the team."*

This is a false statement, too, unless you plan on committing suicide or you live in a society which frowns on failure to an even greater degree than the United States. A form of self-deception, exaggeration will lead you down the path to a Pandora's box of over-inflated disappointment, worry, and anxiety. This may be colorful, passionate language but, in this instance, it is misplaced.

Appropriate language: "If I don't make the team, I'll work harder so I'll have a better chance of making it next year." Or, "I'll ask the coach why I didn't make the team."

E. Question: *"How are you today?"* Answer: *"Not too bad."*

Is "not too bad" anywhere close to "good"? Practice meaningful language. It may be true that you're not too bad or too good, but you have basically told your listener nothing. You may have a cold and feel miserable. Simply express the truth and give it perspective by adding a positive. There is almost always a positive. "I have a cold (true and realistic), but I'm sure happy I don't have the flu like so many of my friends."

Appropriate language: "How are you today?" "I'm a C minus . . . just got some disturbing news from home."

F. *"You think that's bad. Wait 'til you hear about what happened to me!"*

This is one-up-manship. It actively invalidates your experience by implying that her experience is more important than yours. She is thinking about what she is going to say instead of empathetically listening to your story. This is a sign of disrespect.

Appropriate language: None. Be quiet and listen to understand. Then and only then share experience if it is relevant.

F. *Today's forecast: Partly cloudy with occasional snow flurries.*

There is nothing wrong here. This is just a matter of perspective. Practice identifying statements like this if for no other reason than to see a different view of the world. It is partly sunny, too, but I may never see the sun if I focus on "partly cloudy." "Cloudy" is my reality. Changing perspective increases one's creativity. Many great comedians point out the obvious contradictions that exist in our language. Jumbo shrimp (George Carlin). Garage sale . . . want to buy a garage? Physicists have discovered that a wave is a wave if observed one way, and a particle if observed another way.

G. *"I am going to quit drinking alcohol, **totally,** until I lose twenty pounds."*

"I am going to" means I haven't started yet. Start now. There is no reason to delay giving yourself a gift. What happens after the 20 pounds is lost? When you resolve to make a positive change, commit for the duration. Eating and drinking behavior is much like exercise. Positive change yields positive results. Reverting to previous behavior reverts the results as well. Your premium for benefits is never "paid in full." They only last as long as the positive behavior lasts.

Sometimes the thought of giving up something you enjoy for a lifetime triggers feelings of deprivation. It may seem like you need more commitment than you have and you are not ready to pay that much of a price. Two or three months is fine, but a lifetime? Initially, feeling this way is natural, but remember, negativity is natural.

Feelings of deprivation are dangerous because, if they persist, your changes will be short lived. However, they are also positive warnings indicating that your frame of reference needs to be altered. This is relatively easy to do and will occur quickly as you work with nutritional visualization, affirmation statements, and goal setting. Positive change means a better, happier life, not one dispossessed of joy. Take heart if you feel this, though. You are not a failure. You just are not done yet. The purpose of this entire workbook is to help you get "done."

During initial interviews with prospective clients, I tell them that they will reach a point where they will truly *want* nutritious food and *not want* junk food. This may not be a good idea, because some people do *not want* to *not want* donuts!

If you do not want something, you will not be tempted by it. The particular food absolutely loses all of its power. Have you ever felt that the food was in control? Food is inanimate, at least while it's still on the plate. It has no power unless you give it *your* power. Food does not pry the mouth open, chew itself up, and crawl down into the stomach eagerly searching for fat cells to fill up.

What is interesting and exciting is how quickly perception can change. It is another of those phenomena which seem to occur in quantum leaps which is as surprising to the client as it is to me. One client exclaimed with pure delight and amazement, "The boss placed a whole sack full of donuts on my desk and I didn't want one!" He never did *not want* one before. Before, it was the struggle between "good and evil." He wanted one but *should* not have one.

If "good" wins out and he doesn't have one, he still feels badly because he feels deprived. Everyone else is having one. "Why can't I be like Robbie who can eat anything?" Now he has added self-pity to deprivation. If "evil" wins out and he gives in to sensual pleasure, he feels guilty for being weak-willed. So he has another one, which makes him feel better while he is eating it and makes him feel worse when he's finished.

There is a whole array of techniques to counteract streams of uncomfortable, negative thoughts and feelings which occur before, during, and after confrontation with temptation. Through perceptual change, temptation can be eliminated . This in turn eliminates the string of self-perpetuating negativity. There is a very strong camp in the nutrition/weight- reduction field which adamantly maintains that one should never think of any food as "forbidden" food because this sets one up for failure because one cannot help feeling deprived. Diets, therefore, foster binging. I maintain that, with positive perceptual change, forbidden foods are no more than foods we no longer need, want, or crave. They foster nothing. They have no power whatsoever.

I. *"I am going to start my diet right after the holidays."*

Much like the first portion of the previous statement, why delay giving yourself a gift? This is no more than procrastination. It is a way to delay commitment and risk. We get to stay in the comfort zone a little longer. However, the price we pay is delaying the reward of achieving a goal, perhaps forever. We can always find a reason to delay action, to procrastinate.

J. *"My parents always made us clean our plates. We were brought up to 'waste not, want not.'"*

This may very well be a statement of fact. The way one is brought up strongly influences our present behavior. The thing to realize is that, if the behavior fails to nurture our growth, we must take the responsibility to change the behavior regardless of our past, no matter what the past was. The past no longer exists, and we must refuse to excuse present behavior on the basis of the past.

Many therapies dwell on the past to the exclusion of getting on with the present and planning the future. It is as though we analyze the mud we are stuck in to the point of getting more stuck. We may end up with some beautiful mud pies, but we're still in the mud. Sometimes our first need is to just get out of the mud by being willing to leave it behind. Leave the past behind. Do not let your fascination with it hinder you from realizing your potential. Forgiving your parents is as much for your benefit as for theirs. As Fritz Perls stated, "Until you're finished with resentment, you'll never grow up."

K. *"Lordy! I'm stuffed, but this is so-o-o good. Just a few more bites."*

This is an example of alienation from the body. The body is screaming, "I'm full!" You say, "Shut up and enjoy this!" or, "I paid $10.00 for this meal. I'm not going to waste it."

Part of changing perception is learning to listen and act on what the body tells you. If you keep ignoring the signals of the body, you may be like one of my clients who didn't know what hunger felt like. Work on listening to the body with the special technique given in chapter 10.

L. *"I'm big-boned."*

Is this true, or did somebody give you permission to excuse your overfatness? Sometimes someone else will give us permission that we will not give ourselves. As a result, we overlook our potential and our need to grow. Then again, the statement may in fact be true. Be the best big-boned individual you can be and treat it as an asset rather than a liability.

M. *"My husband won't let me work."*

Or, my husband doesn't like skinny women; my husband (spouse) doesn't want me to diet; my spouse this and that, etc.

This statement reveals misplaced responsibility. As an adult, you are responsible for your own growth. Always ask yourself if someone else is fostering or inhibiting your growth. If there is some form of inhibition, you must work to assert your power.

This is a tough one for those who were brought up in an environment where assertion resulted in physical or psychological pain and abuse. As a child, one lacks power and skill. If that was your background, you will probably need some help learning and exercising assertiveness skills unless you are very courageous. It will take time and effort to develop your sense of power.

N. *"I grew up with a German grandma and you know German cooking."*

This is similar to the previous item, "My parents always made us clean our plates. . . ." The statement may be true, and it may help us to understand some of the influences which shaped our present. It will not help us change. Let the past go and do not use it as an excuse for present behavior.

Appropriate language: "I grew up with a German grandma. She was a wonderful cook. She prepared very rich German meals, which I loved."

M. *"Isn't it just awful about Mildred, poor thing?"*

This is an expectation question. I think it is awful about Mildred and I certainly expect you to feel the same. I now have company. We can all perceive life as awful. Again, ask yourself, "Is this really awful?" "What might be worse?" "Is this just my perception?" "What other meanings might be assigned to the event?" Ask Mildred for her meaning.

I heard a nurse say once that nothing is awful unless it is 100-per-cent inconvenient. Even if you are stranded on a surfboard out in the ocean with a shark nibbling at your legs, it is not 100-per-cent inconvenient. He could be eating you more slowly!

Appropriate language: "I feel so sorry for Mildred. I'm going to visit her tomorrow." Or, "I feel badly for Mildred."

P. *"You didn't expect to get that job, did you?"*

This is someone's rather blatant expression of negative expectation accompanied with harsh judgment of your expectation. In essence, you are a fool for expecting the best outcome. It invalidates your judgment.

Appropriate language: "Why do you think you did not get the job?" Or, "Are you disappointed you did not get the job? What will you do now?"

Q. *"All the questions on the math test tomorrow are going to be word problems. I just hate word problems. I'm not good at them."*

Due to past performance, you may know you do poorly on word problems. Expressing or thinking, "I just hate word problems" will only reinforce your distaste. Indulgence in languaging of this kind is extremely difficult to redirect, but it can be accomplished with practice and awareness. Instead of reinforcing the negative, transform the negative to positive language and this will gradually lead to a change in expectation.

Appropriate language: "Word problems are a real challenge for me. I will change my approach and get a tutor to help me." Note: The person is looking for a different solution rather than working harder with the same solution such as, "I'll study harder."

R. *"I'll probably screw it up. I always do."*
Appropriate language: "I will always do my best."

S. *"What'd you expect?"*
Appropriate language: "Did you have fun? Did you play well?"

R and S are similar expectation comments. Expectation is vitally important to visualization techniques and goal setting. Expectation was addressed in these sections.

Appendix B

Experience with Imagery

The following are descriptions of imagery experiences as given by clients, research subjects and workshop participants immediately following guided and self-initiated imagery exercises. Examples of both positive and negative experiences are shared. These examples represent more than 100 people. Also included are questions and concerns commonly expressed by participants.

"I imagined shrinking myself down into a tiny little capsule—like a tiny mini-submarine! I saw that in a movie once. Then I traveled throughout my body seeing the physical reactions taking place. I saw the hypothalamus turning up the metabolism 'dial,' and I sort of rode down and round with the hormones and I literally saw the fat being heated up. An incredible experience. The first few times I didn't see anything at all . . . it took about ten days, but I did the sessions faithfully each day and it worked."

"I saw fat cells 'pop' like bubbles. Then the fat sort of shriveled up with the heat."

"I saw lots of 'yellow' fat, especially around my middle—sort of embedded in my kidneys and intestines. I thought it would be great to actually run and start to loose it. So I did."

Note: This is an example of two-way communication between the body and the mind.

"The fat looked like billowy clouds . . . was trying to reach out and touch it and pull it away."

"Saw what I wanted to be, then went back in [to the hypothalamus] and saw a higher weight but 20 pounds lighter than I am. Which is saying to set one goal at a time."

Note: An example of listening to the wisdom of one's own intuition.

"I imagined hormones coating the fat globules and melting them so it ran in a stream into a furnace and was burned up. Amazing."

"I was having trouble visualizing, so I decided to create my own hypothalamus. I knocked on the door and walked in and saw the gauges. I said to the person in charge I would have to reset them. So we did! What a super feeling. I would never have thought I could have done that, because I'm so logical, not at all creative normally."

"I was in a Venetian gondola floating down the canals. The banks were covered with snow which melted as I passed them. The snow was the fat melting into my blood stream that was carried away and out of my body."

"The fat cells moved passed torches and melted."
"Little men shoveled the fat into furnaces. I smelled

the burning and felt the heat."

"When I went into the hypothalamus there were many workmen. I looked around the room for the foreman and asked for permission to change the controls. After awhile, we were good friends. I no longer had to ask permission."

"When I left the hypothalamus I put a padlock on the door so no one could change it without me knowing about it. I adjusted the controls the first couple of times, but then I didn't have too. It stayed where I wanted it."

Note: Many individuals have indicated that they only go in to check the controls in the hypothalamus after a few imagery-practice sessions. It tends to stay where they want it.

"A lot of Pac-Man™ 'cells' swam about and gobbled up the fat cells."

Note: A "Pac-Man" image is very common.

"The set point was controlled by a machine like a slot machine. I pulled the handle and the weight I wanted to be would show up, each digit on one of the moving dials. 190. But it only stayed there for a moment and the dials would move."

Note: This seems to illustrate the individual's fear of or belief in his lack of control. This is a negative image. He needs to realize that he is in control, at least in his imagination. Since he has the power to manipulate the imagination, he can imagine going in with a mechanic to fix the machine or he can replace the machine with a newer model. There are many possibilities for correcting the problem. It has been suggested by researchers that it may be that some people's mitochondria either don't "turn on" or are defective. Could it be that the body is telling this man that his mitochondria do not function, an example of two-way communication? How would we know? We don't, but he could also imagine his mitochondria burning up excess fat. That way, it is covered.

"Little round fat cells. Back of their heads had a plug which I unplugged. Inner fat was like toothpaste, had to be pushed out by me. Very gross. They had very thick skin. It was a battle."

Note: This is another example of negative imagery. The first part of the imagery, cells with plugs, is acceptable. The last part is symbolic of a psychic struggle. Further, it is symbolically inaccurate at a physiological level. Fat naturally and freely moves in and out of fat cells. She could use the previous sentence as an affirmation. And she needs to change her image to a positive one.

"Set point. Had to keep changing it. Occasionally I could stop it."

Note: This is obviously similar to the image described previously.

"Large box like a safe-set point is the combination but it won't open 'til body is at set point."

Note: Another negative image, this image scenario is from the same woman [above example] who described the fat cells with plugs in their heads. It indicates that she doesn't have the answer, the combination, to control the problem. She needs work on both language and imagery to change her belief and expectation.

"Behind this door is the key to your full potential.

When the door is open a number appears—10 per cent—the door won't open if you cheat, or make bad choices. It's just waiting here for you. Get to work! (Talks to me.)"

"Pituitary gland—little guy speeding up metabolism, generating the system."

"The pituitary and thyroid shoot off hormones like fireworks . . . a Roman candle. Its pretty, very colorful. I feel it shower throughout my body."

"Growth hormone is bright yellow. It flows into the stream [symbolic of blood stream] and mixes with blue thyroxine."

"Fat cells—they were round, greasy and sort of like a hackey sack. The fat cells were white, and firm yet squishy."

"I burned my fat cells by shoveling them up. Sometimes a little man opened the door that contained the fat cells and ordered them out. I felt like a sergeant ordering these fat cells out of me. I could not picture my set point. I couldn't even imagine it."

"When I was asked to burn fat [from the cassette tape], I imagined Superman, like in the movie, quickly flying around the world many, many times. Only, I was running around the world." [He felt warm and was visibly sweating at the end of this session.]
"It was like one of those science films inside my body. I felt the yellow fat melt and disappear and my body got warmer."

"I felt like there was radiation inside my body melting the fat, and the oxygen came in and there was a sort of chemical reaction that gave off heat."

"Feeling of exhilaration when fat is burning."
Note: Exhilaration is a resourceful state. That is, this person very likely feels energized and commitment toward his ideal-weight goal when he is finished with the imagery exercise. He will be able to do what he needs to do to be successful. Who needs cocaine to get a feeling of invincibility?

Concern: "I see the fat melting but there is no place for it to go. It stays in the body."
When fat burns in the presence of carbohydrate, it burns "clean"; that is, there is nothing left in the body. The by-products of fat metabolism are carbon, which combines with oxygen and is exhaled in the form of carbon dioxide, and hydrogen, which combines with oxygen to form water. Water is used for temperature regulation and is eliminated via urine, perspiration, or water vapor in respiration.

Ketones may be a by-product if there is no available carbohydrate. Ketone bodies cause a acidic condition in the body and can be toxic. The body deals with the ketosis by eliminating the ketones through the urine. This requires tremendous amounts of water. Ketosis, therefore, causes dehydration. Water loss as a result of ketosis accounts for the incredibly fast rate of weight loss occurring with low carbohydrate diets. The person loses many pounds, but they are water pounds, not fat pounds.

When you melt a substance such as butter, you have merely changed its physical appearance from solid to liquid. You really do not melt fat in your body. You burn it to create energy in the form of mechanical and heat energy and the by-products of releasing this energy are carbon dioxide, water, and that's it. Unless, of course, you are trying an unsound, dangerous low-carbohydrate diet, in which case you also get ketones, dehydration, and toxicity.

If your vision is one of melting fat, and the melted fat seems stuck in the body, you can change the vision to one of burning fat. Note that in the case of burning fat in the body, the burning is rather slow and not injurious in any way. We do not damage the body with this type of burning. If you melt fat and it disappears— i.e., it isn't "stuck"—go ahead and use the visualization. It will work.

Concern: "I try to get down to my hips and thighs where all the fat is, but all I see is the fat around my heart."

This is a perfect illustration of the fact that visualization is a two-way street. As we attempt to direct the body, the body or mind will sometimes provide us with "intuitive flashes" of what is happening or what is present internally. Because we are relaxed, we have opened up a channel to the right brain wherein reside our intuitive abilities.

I believe intuition is a sense just as sight is. We all experience intuition, but it is a channel of perception that, unlike sight, needs to be and can be developed. Visualization and relaxation activities provide the conditions favorable to intuitive experience because they tend to favor the right side of the brain.

There are many example of intuitive "flashes." I call them flashes because they seem to be of very short duration and one has the distinct feeling that the flash comes instantly, out of nowhere. Its speed and unpredictability distinguish it from a wish or hope or dream.

There was a woman who practiced visualization to help heal her ulcers. She envisioned a group of workmen descending along the route of her alimentary canal, plastering up the holes in the lining of her intestine and stomach much like one would plaster up a hole in a ceiling. She practiced twice a day for two weeks. A member of the medical staff showed her the x-rays so that she could see where the ulcers were.

Upon examining the x-rays, she said she already knew where the ulcers were. After all, she had been plastering up the holes twice a day for two weeks!

Concern: "I can see myself before the mirror, all right. But I can't seem to get down into my body."

Emphasize surrender, patience, waiting in silence. Remember, it is when we finally give up trying that the imagination surprises us most. This is a rather common experience. Many examples exist in the literature illustrating this experience among writers or scientists. They concentrate hours upon hours on a problem and the solution comes during a period of exhaustion or a brief period of rest. In a flash the parts of the puzzle come together in the "Aha!" experience. The light bulb goes on, the intuitive flash. The "Aha" probably would not have happened without the previous labor. The key is persistence and patience. You never know when the experience will happen.

> Failure I may still encounter at the thousandth step, yet success hides behind the next bend in the road. . . . I will persist until I succeed.
> —Og Mandino

Concern: "I just go crazy trying to sit still to do visualization. I get very restless and I can't sit there another minute."

My first suggestion is that you try several sessions to sit through it another minute, actually 15 to 20 minutes, even if your mind wanders continuously. Part of the restlessness is a matter of being undisciplined. With commitment, tenacity, and concentration, you can become disciplined. Most people in this culture are on the go continually and to sit in silence and "let" something happen is very different from sitting down to be entertained. It is amazing that we can sit in front of a television set from four to six hours a day and be perfectly comfortable (or mesmerized), and yet to sit down to silence for our own minds to create the vision for two sessions of 20 minutes is unnerving! Sometimes I think we are afraid of ourselves. So, forego the television for 40 minutes a day and risk the silence. It is a different kind of adventure but, in fact, it is a more thrilling one, because you grow as a result instead of stagnating.

Now, if you have given it a fair trial, then do as previously suggested. Stand up and move around a bit. You will find that, as you become more skilled and practiced at the art of imagery, you will automatically use it under a vast variety of situations and conditions, in the shower, while working out, driving, mowing the lawn, and even carrying on conversations on topics unrelated to the vision.

References

Introduction

Viscott, David. *Language of Feelings*. New York: Pocket Books, 1976, quoted in Sinetar, Marsha. *Do Want You Love the Money Will Follow*. New York: Paulist Press, 1987, p. 66.

Sinetar, Marsha. *Do Want You Love the Money Will Follow*. New York: Paulist Press, 1987, p. 48.

Bandler, Richard, and Grinder, John. *Frogs into Princes*. Moab, Utah, Real People Press, 1979, p. 12-13.

Frankl, Victor. *Man's Search for Meaning*. New York: Washington Square Press, 1984.

Dhjarma teaching, Insight Meditation Center, Barre, MA, 1983 quoted in Vaughan, Frances. *The Inward Arc*. Boston: New Science Library Shambhala, 1986, p. 15.

Siegel, Bernie S. *Love, Medicine & Miracles*. New York: Harper & Row, Publishers, 1986.

Zukav, Gary. *The Dancing Wu Li Masters*. New York: Bantam Books, 1979, p. 33.

Simonton, O. Carl, Matthews-Simonton, Stephanie, and Creighton, James. *Getting Well Again.* Los Angeles, 1978, p. 29.

Kirk, Constance C. The Effects of Guided Imagery on Basal Metabolic Rate, *Journal of the Society for Accelerated Learning and Teaching,* 13(4), 1988, pp. 347-362.

Mandino, Og. *The Greatest Salesman in the World.* New York: Bantam Books, 1968, p. 65.

Part 1: Languaging:
Hammarskjold, Dag. *Markings.* London: Faber and Faber, 1964, p. 36.

Chapter 1: Languaging: The Key to Unlocking Limitless Possibilities
Csikszentmihalyi, Mihaly. *Flow: The Psychology of Optimal Experience.* New York: Harper & Row, 1990, p. 34.

Hill, Napoleon. *Think and Grow Rich.* New York: Fawcett Crest Books, 1960, p. 67.

Orr, Leonard and Ray, Sondra. *Rebirthing in the New Age.* Berkeley, CA: Celestial Arts, 1983. Discussion of personal laws is addressed in Orr's Money Seminar tapes.

Chapter 2: Designer Affirmations
Rico, Gabriele Lusser. *Writing the Natural Way.* Los Angeles: J.P. Tarcher, Inc., 1983.

Chapter 3: Goal Setting

Blanchard, Kenneth and Johnson, Spencer. *The One Minute Manager*. New York: William Morrow and Company, Inc., 1982, p. 97.

Csikszentmihalyi, Mihaly. Flow: *The Psychology of Optimal Experience*. New York: Harper & Row, 1990, p. 34.

Mandingo, Og. *The Greatest Success in the World*. New York: Bantam Books, 1981, pp. 76-77.

Chapter 4: The Working Ideal: Building Motivational Muscle.

Glasser, William. *Control Theory in the Classroom*. New York: Harper & Row, Publisher, 1986, p.17.

Puryear, Herbert. *The Edgar Cayce Primer*. New York: Bantam Books, 1982, p. 15.

Part 2: Imagery

Lopez, Barry quote in Fox, Matthew. *Original Blessing*. Santa Fe, NM: Bear & Company, Inc., 1983, p. 178

Tart, Charles T. *Waking Up*. Boston: New Science Library Shambhala, 1987, p. 59.

Chapter 5: Imagery: The Power Source

Samuels, Mike and Samuels, Nancy. *Seeing with the Mind's Eye*. New York: Random House, 1975, p. xii.

Simonton, O. Carl, Matthews-Simonton, Stephanie, and Creighton, James. *Getting Welling Again*. Los Angeles: J. P. Tarcher, Inc., 1978, p. 29.

Brown, Barbara. *Super-Mind.* New York: Harper & Row, Publishers, Inc., 1980, p. 254.

Chapter 6: Levels of Imagery
Rico, Gabriele Lusser. *Writing the Natural Way.* Los Angeles: J. P. Tarcher, Inc., 1983.

Kirk, Constance C. The Effects of Guided Imagery on Basal Metabolic Rate, *Journal of the Society for Accelerated Learning and Teaching,* 13(4), 1988, pp. 347-362.

Chapter 7: Assets and Liabilities
Watts, Alan. *The Wisdom of Insecurity.* New York: Vintage Books, 1951, p. 24.

Hill, Napoleon. *Think & Grow Rich.* New York: Fawcett Crest Books, 1960, p. 40.

Part 3: Experience
Milne, A. A. *Winnie-the-Pooh.* New York: E. P. Dutton, 1961, p. 160.

Chapter 9: Savoring
Kushner, Harold. *When All You Ever Wanted Isn't Enough.* New York: Pocket Books, 1986, p. 145-146.

_____p. 142.

Fox, Matthew. *Original Blessing.* Santa Fe, NM: Bear & Company, Inc., 1983, p. 52.

Campbell, Joseph, and Flowers, Betty Sue (Ed.) *The Power of Myth with Bill Moyers*. New York: Doubleday, 1988, p. 3.

Chapter 10: Listening to the Body

Progoff, Ira. *At a Journal Workshop*. New York: Dialogue House Library, 1975, p. 202.

Slochower, Joyce Anne. *Excessive Eating: The Role of Emotions and Environment*. New York: Human Science Press, 1983, p. 13

Rose, Colin. *The Mind & Body Diet*. Bucks., United Kingdom: Aston Clinton, 1989, pp. 49-50.

Appendix B

Mandino, Og, *The Greatest Salesman in the World*. New York: Bantam, 1968, p 64.

STAY IN TOUCH

On the following pages you will find listed, with their current prices, some of the books now available on related subjects. Your book dealer stocks most of these, and will stock new titles in the Llewellyn series as they become available. We urge your patronage.

However, to obtain our full catalog, to keep informed of new titles as they are released and to benefit from informative articles and helpful news, you are invited to write for our bi-monthly news magazine/catalog. A sample copy is free, and it will continue coming to you at no cost as long as you are an active mail customer. Or you may keep it coming for a full year with a donation of just $5.00 in U.S.A. & Canada ($20.00 overseas, first class mail). Many bookstores also have *The Llewellyn New Times* available to their customers. Ask for it.

Stay in touch! In *The Llewellyn New Times'* pages you will find news and reviews of new books, tapes and services, announcements of meetings and seminars, articles helpful to our readers, news of authors, advertising of products and services, special money-making opportunities, and much more.

The Llewellyn New Times
P.O. Box 64383-Dept. 372, St. Paul, MN 55164-0383, U.S.A.

• • •

TO ORDER BOOKS AND TAPES

If your book dealer does not have the books described on the following pages readily available, you may order them direct from the publisher by sending full price in U.S. funds, plus $1.50 for postage and handling for orders *under* $10.00; $3.00 for orders *over* $10.00. There are no postage and handling charges for orders over $50.00. UPS Delivery: We ship UPS whenever possible. Delivery guaranteed. Provide your street address as UPS does not deliver to P.O. Boxes. UPS to Canada requires a $50.00 minimum order. Allow 4–6 weeks for delivery. Orders outside the U.S.A. and Canada: Airmail—add retail price of book; add $5.00 for each non-book item (tapes, etc.); add $1.00 per item for surface mail.

FOR GROUP STUDY AND PURCHASE

Because there is a great deal of interest in group discussion and study of the subject matter of this book, we feel that we should encourage the adoption and use of this particular book by such groups by offering a special "quantity" price to group leaders or "agents."

Our Special Quantity Price for a minimum order of five copies of *Taming the Diet Dragon* is $23.85 cash-with-order. This price includes postage and handling within the United States. Minnesota residents must add 6.5% sales tax. For additional quantities, please order in multiples of five. For Canadian and foreign orders, add postage and handling charges as above. Credit card (VISA, Master Card, American Express) orders are accepted. Charge card orders only may be phoned free ($15.00 minimum order) within the U.S.A. or Canada by dialing 1-800-THE-MOON. Customer service calls dial 1-612-291-1970. Mail Orders to:

LLEWELLYN PUBLICATIONS
P.O. Box 64383-Dept. 372 / St. Paul, MN 55164-0383, U.S.A.

Prices subject to change without notice.

JUDE'S HERBAL HOME REMEDIES
Natural Health, Beauty & Home-Care Secrets
by Jude C. Williams, M.H.

There's a pharmacy—in your spice cabinet! In the course of daily life we all encounter problems that can be easily treated through the use of common herbs—headaches, dandruff, insomnia, colds, muscle aches, burns—and a host of other afflictions known to humankind. *Jude's Herbal Home Remedies* is a simple guide to self care that will benefit beginner or experienced herbalists with its wealth of practical advice.

Ms. Williams explores the gamut of natural healing with recipes and preparations for beauty; hair care; skin problems; colds and chest complaints; digestive ailments; ear, eye, nose and throat problems; headaches and nervous disorders; wounds; arthritis, and much more.

Build a better-balanced relationship with nature and your inner self—while saving money along the way.

0-87542-869-X, 240 pgs., 6 x 9, illus., softcover   **$9.95**

HERB MAGIC VIDEO
by and featuring Scott Cunningham

Herb Magic, written by and featuring Scott Cunningham, gives the clearest view ever of how to do magic with herbs!

- Watch Scott prepare magical oils, sachets, incenses, and more.
- Visit a large, working herb farm.
- Learn to identify common herbs in their natural surroundings.
- Discover and use the power of herb magic and spells—secrets that are revealed here for the very first time.
- Learn to make flower and herb essences, oils, and tinctures for use as magical tools, bath oils or perfumes.

In this hour-long video, Scott presents many recipes and spells which use herbs. On this tape Scott gives specific, in-depth instructions on harvesting and preparing herbs for magical purposes. It is often easier to learn something by having it demonstrated to you than it is when you read about it in a book. With this videotape Cunningham gives you a personal lesson in herb magic!

0-87542-117-2, VHS, 60 min.   **$29.95**

Prices subject to change without notice.

THE COMPLETE HANDBOOK OF NATURAL HEALING
by Marcia Starck

Now, all the information that has been uncovered during the holistic health movement is compiled in this one volume in concise and usable form. With this book you will acquaint yourself with the variety of natural therapies available as well as heal yourself and your family of most ailments.

Designed to function as a home reference guide (yet enjoyable and interesting enough to read straight through), this book addresses all natural healing modalities in use today: dietary regimes, nutritional supplements, cleansing and detoxification, vitamins and minerals, herbology, homeopathic medicine and cell salts, traditional Chinese medicine, Ayurvedic medicine, body work therapies, exercise, mental and spiritual therapies, subtle and vibrational healing, and diagnostic techniques. A section of 41 specific ailments outlines all natural treatments for everything from insect bites to varicose veins to AIDS.

0-87542-742-1, 384 pgs., 6 x 9, diagrams, softcover **$12.95**

THE ART OF SPIRITUAL HEALING
by Keith Sherwood

Each of you has the potential to be a healer; to heal yourself and to become a channel for healing others. Healing energy is always flowing through you. Learn how to recognize and tap this incredible energy source. You do not need to be a victim of disease or poor health. Rid yourself of negativity and become a channel for positive healing.

Become acquainted with your three auras and learn how to recognize problems and heal them on a higher level before they become manifested in the physical body as disease.

Special techniques make this book a "breakthrough" to healing power, but you are also given a concise, easy-to-follow regimen of good health to follow in order to maintain a superior state of being. This is a practical guide to healing.

0-87542-720-0, 256 pgs., 5-1/4 x 8, illus., softcover **$7.95**

Prices subject to change without notice.

THE SECRET OF LETTING GO
by Guy Finley

Whether you need to let go of a painful heartache, a destructive habit, a frightening worry or a nagging discontent, *The Secret of Letting Go* shows you how to call upon your own hidden powers and how they can take you through and beyond any challenge or problem. This book reveals the secret source of a brand-new kind of inner strength.

In the light of your new and higher self-understanding, emotional difficulties such as loneliness, fear, anxiety and frustration fade into nothingness as you happily discover they never really existed in the first place.

With a foreword by Desi Arnaz, Jr., and introduction by Dr. Jesse Freeland, *The Secret of Letting Go* is a pleasing balance of questions and answers, illustrative examples, truth tales, and stimulating dialogues that allow the reader to share in the exciting discoveries that lead up to lasting self-liberation.

This is a book for the discriminating, intelligent, and sensitive reader who is looking for *real* answers.

0-87542-223-3, 272 pgs., 5 -1/4 x 8, softcover $9.95

WHAT YOUR DREAMS CAN TEACH YOU
by Alex Lukeman

Dreams are honest and do not lie. They have much to teach us, but the lessons are often difficult to understand. Confusion comes not from the dream but from the outer mind's attempt to understand it.

What Your Dreams Can Teach You is a workbook of self-discovery, with a systematic and proven approach to the understanding of dreams. It does *not* contain lists of meanings for dream symbols. Only you, the dreamer, can discover what the images in your dreams mean for you. The book *does* contain step-by-step information which can lead you to success with your dreams, success that will bear fruit in your waking hours. Learn to tap into the aspect of yourself that truly knows how to interpret dreams, the inner energy of understanding called the "Dreamer Within." This aspect of your consciousness will lead you to an accurate understanding of your dreams and even assist you with interpreting dreams of others.

0-87542-475-9, 288 pgs., 6 x 9, illus., softcover $12.95

Prices subject to change without notice.